STUDIES IN ECONOMICS AND BUSINESS

KW-053-661

UK Current
Economic Policy

Second Edition

David Smith

Series Editor
Susan Grant
West Oxfordshire College

Heinemann

Heinemann Educational Publishers
Halley Court, Jordan Hill, Oxford OX2 8EJ
a division of Reed Educational & Professional Publishing Ltd

OXFORD MELBOURNE AUCKLAND
JOHANNESBURG BLANTYRE GABORONE
IBADAN PORTSMOUTH (NH) USA CHICAGO

Heinemann is a registered trademark of Reed Educational & Professional Publishing Ltd

First published in 1994 in the Studies in the UK Economy series.
Second edition published 1999

03 02 01 00 99
10 9 8 7 6 5 4 3 2 1

British Library Cataloguing in Publication Data
A catalogue record for this book is available from the British Library

ISBN 0 431 02974 1

Typeset and illustrated by TechType, Abingdon, Oxon.
Printed and bound in Great Britain by Biddles Ltd, Guildford

Acknowledgements
The publishers would like to thank the following for permission to reproduce copyright
material:

AEB for the questions on pp. 39, 52; Daily Record for the extract on p. 101; Dataset for the material
on p. 40; Datastream for the charts on pp. 87, 110; *The Economist* for the extract on p. 40, © *The
Economist*, London (4/9/93); Edexcel Foundation for the questions on pp. 11, 39–41, 52, 78, 117;
The Evening Standard/Solo Syndication for the extract on p. 46; HMSO for the material on pp. 4, 9,
14, 20, 22, 27, 28, 42, 49, 54, 55, 67, 68, 70, 72, 76, 81, 83, 91, 95, 102, 105, 106: Crown copyright
is reproduced with the permission of the Controller of Her Majesty's Stationery Office; *The
Independent* for the extract from 'Millions are ready to veto with their hearts on unemployment', by
Diana Coyle, *The Independent*, 7/3/96, on pp. 65-6; Lloyds Bank Group Economic Research for the
extract from 'EMU to make uncertain start', by Patrick Foley, Lloyds Bank Economic Bulletin, no. 19,
February 1998, on p. 117–19; OCR for the questions on pp. 11–13, 24–6, 52–3, 65–6, 78–80, 93–4,
104–5; OECD Publications for the graphs on pp. 58, 82, © OECD 1996, 1999; The Office for
National Statistics for the material on pp. 12, 94, 97; Dave Simonds for the cartoon on p. 75;
Telegraph Group Limited for the articles 'Taxes are set to rise, admits Blair', *The Daily Telegraph*,
4/3/99 and 'UK Productivity: Economic Agenda', *The Sunday Telegraph*, 29/11/98, on pp. 15, 86;
Times Newspapers Ltd/News International Syndication for the extracts from *The Sun* on p. 115 (©
Times Newspapers 24/6/98), from *The Times* on p. 59 (© Times Newspapers Ltd (1/2/99), and from
The Sunday Times on pp. 25, 29, 73 (© Times Newspapers 30/8/98, 19/7/98, 22/3/92).

The publishers have made every effort to contact copyright holders. However, if any material has
been incorrectly acknowledged, the publishers would be pleased to correct this at the earliest
opportunity.

*For more information about Heinemann Library books, or to order, please phone 01865 888066,
or send a fax to 01865 314091. You can visit our web site at www.heinemann.co.uk.

Contents

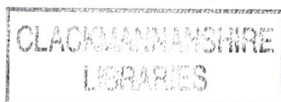

Preface

This is an eagerly awaited new edition of David Smith's popular book. As in the previous edition and in his other books and column for the *Sunday Times*, David Smith writes with considerable authority and clarity.

This new edition examines the key features, and roles, of the microeconomic and macroeconomic policies of the government. It discusses how the government is seeking to achieve its objectives via greater stability in government policy, including the new relationship between the administration and the Bank of England, and the government's fiscal policy rules.

Susan Grant
Series Editor

Introduction

This second edition of *UK Current Economic Policy* is actually the fourth edition in a sequence which began life as *Mrs Thatcher's Economics* in the 1980s; that book evolved into *Mrs Thatcher's Economics: Her Legacy*, which became the first edition of *UK Current Economic Policy*. Each book has been different from its predecessor, none more so than this one.

After 18 years in opposition, the Labour party took office in May 1997 determined to radically reform the economic policy process, most dramatically with the granting of operational independence – the power of setting interest rates – to the Bank of England. This change, within days of the general election, was but one of many. If you were to characterize the Labour government's approach it would be that, whereas in the past Labour chancellors of the exchequer soon found themselves bogged down in short-term economic management, and in particular sterling crises, this one was determined to minimize that risk, and concentrate on raising Britain's long-run economic performance and making a reality of its election slogan of offering 'equality of opportunity'.

The fact that economic policy has changed so much in the past 15 years is what makes the subject a fascinating one to study. Economics is a living subject. A few years ago, economists advised while politicians took the decisions. Now, with the Bank of England's monetary policy committee, we have a living example of economists taking decisions which influence the everyday lives. Anybody who doubts whether economics is worth studying should bear this example in mind.

- **About this book**

In the following nine chapters, I describe the main areas of economic policy and the theory which lies behind them. In some cases there is room to provide only a brief introduction into a subject area, and I would urge students to read further, using the references at the end of each chapter, as well as the various websites listed. I would also, for obvious reasons, urge regular reading of the economics articles in newspapers and magazines, particularly, of course, my own contributions in the *Sunday Times* (www.sunday-times.co.uk). You can also read my monthly columns in *Management Today* (www.bestpractice.haynet.com).

Chapter 1 is about the role and limits of economic policy. It starts with the question: What is economic policy? It then touches on growth, inflation and unemployment; the three ways of measuring gross domestic product; macroeconomic and microeconomic policy; aggregate demand and supply; objectives and instruments; and the modern response to the policy conflict.

Chapter 2 is about taxation: the tax burden; types of taxation; the principles of taxation; taxation, incentives and the supply side; the Laffer curve; tax cuts and the work/leisure trade-off; taxation and the distribution of income.

Chapter 3 covers public expenditure and the changing role of fiscal policy: fiscal policy; the modern welfare state; debts and deficits; deficits and 'crowding out'; the comprehensive spending review; the case for and against privatization; privatization and regulation;the National Asset Register.

Chapter 4 looks at the Bank of England and monetary policy. What is monetary policy and how does it work? It covers monetarism and the money supply; Bank of England independence (Is independence better?) and the inflation target; how Bank independence compares with other countries.

Chapter 5 is about employment. It covers the measurement of unemployment; traditional full employment (Whatever happened to it?); voluntary and involuntary unemployment; the unemployment/ inflation trade-off (the Phillips curve); the natural rate and the NAIRU; and modern 'full employment'.

Chapter 6 is about stability and economic growth: the business cycle; business-cycle theories; traditional counter-cyclical policies; Britain's cyclical experience; whether cyclical volatility reduces economic growth; and government policies for stability.

Chapter 7 looks at productivity and competition. What is productivity? Why does Britain lag behind? What policies can be used to boost productivity? Is there a trade-off between productivity and employment? Does competition boost productivity?

Chapter 8 examines devolution and regional policy: the regional problem; the rise and fall of regional policy; devolution; and the economics of independence.

Chapter 9 looks at Britain in Europe: the UK and the European Union; customs unions and common markets; European economic and monetary union; Britain, the ERM and 'Black Wednesday'; achieving EMU; the pros and cons of EMU; and Britain and the euro.

It may be that, by the time this book comes to be revised again, Britain will be part of the single currency and a further sea change will have occurred in UK economic policymaking. Until that happens, I hope this book will assist you, and I wish you every success.

Chapter One

The role and limits of economic policy

'It is the conquest of inflation, and not the pursuit of growth and employment, which is or should be the objective of macroeconomic policy. And it is the creation of conditions conducive to growth and employment, and not the suppression of price rises, which is or should be the objective of microeconomic policy.'
Nigel Lawson (as Chancellor of the Exchequer), Mais Lecture 1984

What is economic policy?

Most people would define economic policy as the core activities of a modern-day Chancellor of the Exchequer, together with those actions taken on behalf of the government by the Bank of England. Thus it includes decisions on:

- taxation – both the overall level and rates for individual taxes
- public expenditure – including the way it is divided between programmes, and between current and capital spending
- interest rates, and the growth of money and credit
- the external value of sterling, and whether it is fixed, floating, or intended to be part of the European single currency.

This, however, would be only a narrow definition of economic policy. When governments act to raise educational standards this has an effect, over the long term, on the nation's economic performance. A better educated workforce is usually a more productive one. The same is true for health. Investment in roads and the railways improves economic efficiency. Few actions of government do not affect the economy in some way.

No clear boundary exists at which economic policy stops and other policies begin. But it is necessary, in this book, to set some limits, specifically that of *defining economic policy as those actions by government whose intentions are mainly economic.*

Growth, inflation and unemployment

Let us begin with some basic definitions. When economists talk of economic growth, they mean the rate of growth of **gross domestic product** (GDP). This is measured in three ways. It is the sum total of all incomes and production in the economy, and all expenditures and goods produced in the economy. The totals should add up to the same overall figure, although in practice there is usually a significant statistical discrepancy. Table 1 shows the GDP, measured on the expenditure basis, for the UK in 1998.

Table 1 is useful because it sets out what is known as the 'national income identity'. GDP (sometimes called 'national income') is equal to private consumption plus government consumption plus investment plus any change in inventories (or stocks) plus exports, *less* imports. If we think of the two other ways of measuring GDP, income and production, we can see why this identity holds. Anything that is spent in Britain, together with anything that is spent by foreigners on British goods and services (exports), adds to British income and the value of British production. But anything that is produced abroad and sold here (imports) does not, and so has to be deducted to give our GDP figure.

Note that the table refers to GDP in 1995 prices. To measure the economy's growth rate, it is necessary to remove the inflation component from GDP. Otherwise periods of high inflation would wrongly appear to be periods of high growth. Adjusting for inflation in this way is known as 'deflating' GDP and the overall measure of inflation used to do this is called the **GDP deflator**.

The more common measure of inflation is, however, that which is measured by the **retail price index**, or RPI. The government targets inflation according to a slightly different measure, the RPI excluding mortgage interest payments, or **RPIX**. The target for the latter is currently 2.5 per cent, although at some stage the government plans to switch to a new target based on the so-called harmonized index of

Table 1 GDP (expenditure measure) at 1995 prices (£ billion)

Household consumption	505.4
General government consumption	146.2
Fixed investment	137.7
Change in inventories	6.9
Domestic demand (the sum of the above)	796.2
Exports, goods and services	243.5
Total final expenditure (all the above)	**1039.7**
Less imports, goods and services	262.7
Equals GDP at market prices	**776.9**

Source: HM Treasury, Pre-budget report, November 1998

consumer prices (HICP), which uses the same method of calculation as other countries in Europe.

Two other important statistical variables are **unemployment** and the **balance of payments**. Unemployment has traditionally been measured by the claimant count – the number of people unemployed and claiming benefit. More recently the government has indicated that its preferred measure of unemployment is based on the Labour Force Survey, which includes people who are eligible for work but not entitled to benefit. In early 1999, unemployment was 1.3 million on the claimant count and 1.7 million of the LFS measure.

The balance of payments consists of two elements, the **current account** and the capital account. The two normally balance out: a country running a current account deficit – based on trade in goods and services plus other 'invisible' items of trade such as investment income from abroad and the City's earnings – requires a compensating inflow on the capital account.

Macroeconomic and microeconomic policy

Macroeconomic policy includes taxation and public spending, which together make up **fiscal policy**. Interest rates and the exchange rate are the key elements of **monetary policy**. Macroeconomic policy can also include *incomes policies*, which attempt to limit overall pay rises; *trade policy*, where Britain has favoured freeing international trade under the auspices of first the GATT (the General Agreement on Tariffs and Trade) and now the WTO (World Trade Organization); and *regional policy*, intended to influence the distribution of economic activity between regions.

Microeconomic policy consists of actions aimed at improving the economy's long-term growth potential, by acting on the **supply side**. Examples are:

- improving incentives for workers and entrepreneurs
- increasing and improving the supply of labour through government training schemes and welfare reform
- outlawing restrictive practices
- increasing competition
- ensuring that the financial system is an efficient supplier of finance for business expansion.

Modern microeconomic policy tries to raise economic efficiency by improving the workings of markets.

One way of characterizing the economic approach of the Labour government elected in May 1997 is that the Chancellor of the Exchequer, Gordon Brown, attempted to reduce the emphasis on day-to-day macroeconomic management, by granting operational independence to the Bank of England (control of interest rates) and by setting fiscal policy, both tax and public spending, in a medium-term context. That way, it was said, there could be a greater emphasis on microeconomic measures to improve long-run performance.

Macroeconomic policy, aggregate demand and aggregate supply

One common way of thinking about how macroeconomic policy operates is by means of **aggregate demand** and **aggregate supply**. An aggregate demand curve shows the overall level of demand in the economy for a series of price levels. As with a normal demand curve, the lower the price level the greater the demand. With an expansionary macroeconomic policy, for example, an increase in government spending has the effect of increasing aggregate demand at each price level. It pushes the aggregate demand curve outwards, from AD to AD_1 (see Figure 1).

To assess the overall impact of macroeconomic policy on the economy, it is necessary to introduce aggregate supply – the overall amount of goods and services supplied at each price level. Traditional **Keynesian** analysis assumed that, until full capacity in the economy was reached, governments could expand demand, and reduce unemployment, without increasing the price level. The assumption was

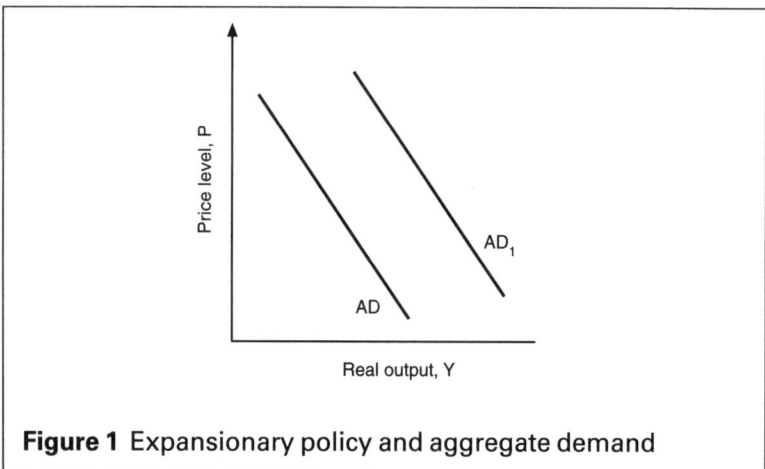

Figure 1 Expansionary policy and aggregate demand

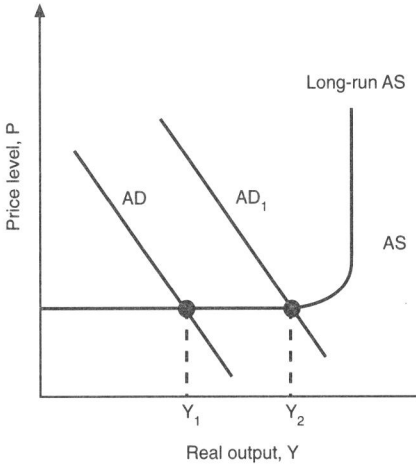

Figure 2 Aggregate demand and 'Keynesian' aggregate supply

of an aggregate supply curve which was horizontal until the point of full capacity (and full employment) was reached, whereupon it would become vertical – and further expansion of demand by the government would result only in higher prices. This is shown in Figure 2.

The shift in the aggregate demand curve from from AD to AD_1 has the effect of pushing real output from Y_1 to Y_2, without affecting the price level. Thus, it seemed, governments should introduce expansionary policies until they achieved full employment – the point at which the AS curve becomes vertical.

Modern new classical (or **neoclassical**) economists, however, do not believe the aggregate supply curve is of this 'Keynesian' type. Examine Figure 3.

Figure 3 is a little more complicated. It shows, first, two *short-run* aggregate supply curves, AS and AS_1. When the government takes steps to expand aggregate demand from AD to AD_1, the initial response is to produce a shift along the aggregate supply curve AS. Firms see both an increase in demand and higher prices, from P_1 to P_2 (which they initially believe applies only to the goods they produce). They increase production, raising the level of national output (Y) from Y_1 to Y_2, and reducing the level of unemployment.

This is, however, only the first stage. Because the increase in aggregate demand pushes up not just the prices faced by individual firms but also

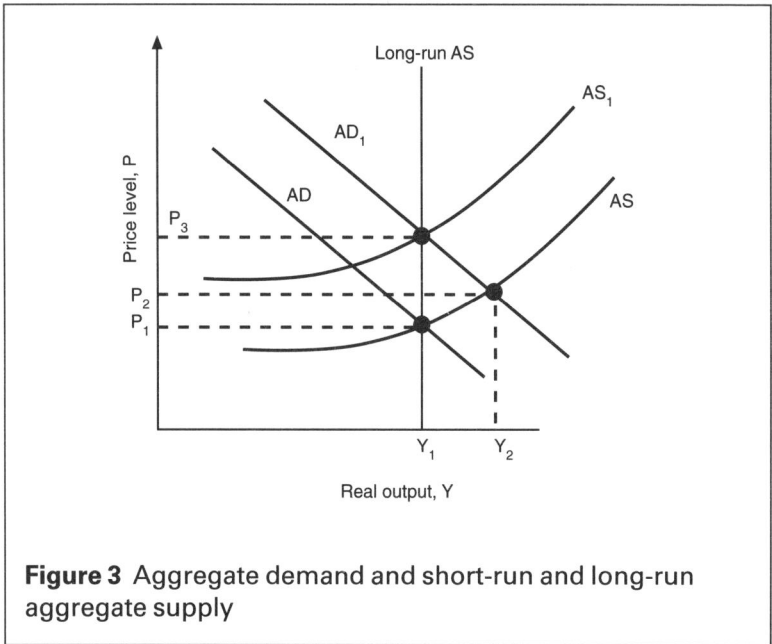

Figure 3 Aggregate demand and short-run and long-run aggregate supply

the general price level, the effect is to produce an increase in money wage rates (workers demand an increase in wages to compensate for higher prices). Once firms are faced with the need to pay higher money wages, the amount they are willing to supply at each price level falls. The aggregate supply curve shifts to the left, from AS to AS_1.

This then gives us our long-run aggregate supply curve, which as the chart shows is vertical. *An increase in aggregate demand as a result of expansionary government policy results in only a temporary increase in output.* Supply-side policies are needed to raise the level of output over the long run – by shifting the long-run AS schedule to the right. Otherwise, expansionary policies result only in higher prices – the final price level is P_3.

Objectives and instruments

Even allowing for this, economic policy does not sound that difficult. Governments just have to make sure that all aspects of policy are geared towards achieving the same **objectives**. These are:

● achievement of the fastest sustainable growth for gross domestic product (GDP)
● the highest possible level of employment

- stable prices (or at least low inflation, for example the current 2.5 per cent target)
- external balance – ensuring the current account of the balance of payments is not in large deficit
- sound public finance – for example the '**golden rule**' of using only public borrowing to finance public investment over the economic cycle.

Governments use **instruments** of policy to achieve these objectives. Macroeconomic policies to boost economic growth include expansionary fiscal policy (reduced taxation and increased government spending) and a relaxation of monetary policy, through lower interest rates and a falling exchange rate. But expanding fiscal policy will mean a bigger budget deficit (or public sector net cash requirement), while lowering both interest rates and the exchange rate would, in normal circumstances, boost inflation.

The government's economic approach

The government's central objective is to achieve high and stable levels of growth and employment, goals which have proved elusive in the past. In meeting this objective, the government wants to encourage a fair society in which everyone can share in higher living standards and greater job opportunities, and to see economic development taking place in a way which respects the environment. Achieving these aims in the new global economy will require a major re-equipping of the British economy.

In working towards its aims, the government is putting in place a comprehensive and consistent set of economic policies designed to:

- *improve the underlying rate of growth and employment* by:
  (a) creating economic stability based on low inflation and low government borrowing
  (b) improving the environment for long-term investment in technology and in education and training
  (c) encouraging a climate of entrepreneurship and competition
- *modernize the welfare state* so that it provides an effective way of supporting people back into work rather than trapping them in poverty
- *ensure high-quality public services* are delivered in the most effective way
- *develop a tax system which is fair* and seen to be fair
- *ensure that economic development takes place* in a way which is consistent with high standards of environmental protection.

Source: Financial Statement and Budget Report, HM Treasury, July 1997

The problem for policymakers is that it is not possible to assign separate policy instruments to the different objectives of policy, and governments typically have more policy objectives than instruments. Jan Tinbergen, a Dutch economist, formulated a 'rule' under which it was necessary to have as many independent policy instruments as objectives. This is why governments have in the past tried to invent new instruments (e.g. prices and incomes policies) which attempt to control inflation directly, in an effort to square the circle.

A bigger problem is that policy instruments operate simultaneously on a number of different targets. A lower exchange rate might be the right policy for achieving balance of payments equilibrium, but it will also (by raising the price of imports) add to inflation.

The modern response to the policy conflict

Modern governments have tried to solve the conflict inherent in objectives and instruments by limiting the scope of macroeconomic policy. The central aim has been to use macroeconomic policy to control inflation, while concentrating the microeconomic policy effort on raising economic growth.

As this approach has been refined, so inflation has come to be the only policy objective which is specifically targeted. Treasury ministers have stressed that the control of inflation has to be the main objective of policy. Without it, growth will inevitably run into the brick wall of an unsustainable balance-of-payments position (British goods become uncompetitive in international markets), and an inevitable tightening of policy to re-establish control over inflation. Low inflation is thus seen as a necessary condition for the achievement of the other objectives. There is no long-run trade-off, in other words, between growth and inflation.

Even with this approach, however, there are compromises. The government does not target zero inflation, but a rate of 2.5 per cent. It also attempts to ensure that the Bank of England does not engage in policy 'overkill'. The Bank is required to explain its actions if inflation falls below 1.5 per cent.

Economic policy, therefore, has to strive to establish a balance between various objectives. Compromises are inevitable, perfection is rarely achieved. If economics is about the allocation of scarce resources, *economic policy is the allocation of scarce policy instruments between competing, and often conflicting, ends.*

```
┌─────────────────────────────────────────────────────────┐
│                      KEY WORDS                            │
│                                                           │
│  Gross domestic product       Microeconomic policy        │
│  GDP deflator                 Supply side                 │
│  Retail price index           Aggregate demand            │
│  RPIX                         Aggregate supply            │
│  Unemployment                 Keynesian                   │
│  Balance of payments          Neoclassical                │
│  Current account              Objectives                  │
│  Macroeconomic policy         'Golden rule'               │
│  Fiscal policy                Instruments                 │
│  Monetary policy                                          │
└─────────────────────────────────────────────────────────┘
```

Further reading

Artis, M. (ed), Chapter 5 in *The UK Economy*, 14th edn, Oxford University Press, 1996.

Beardshaw, J. *et al.*, Chapters 43 and 47 in *Economics: A Student's Guide*, 4th edn, Addison-Wesley Longman, 1998.

Griffiths, A. and Wall, S., Chapter 17 in *Applied Economics*, 7th edn, Addison-Wesley Longman, 1997.

Sloman, J., Chapters 13 and 14 in *Economics*, 3rd edn, Prentice Hall, 1997.

Useful website

HM Treasury: www.hm-treasury.gov.uk/

Essay topics

1. (a) Which *two* objectives of macroeconomic policy do you consider to be the most important for the UK to pursue in the first decade of the twenty-first century? Justify your answer. [40 marks]
   (b) Explain how these objectives might conflict with one another and with other macroeconomic goals. [60 marks] [University of London Examinations and Assessment Council 1996 (adapted)]
2. Discuss why a government's macroeconomic objectives conflict with each other and suggest ways in which these conflicts might be reduced. [40 marks] [University of Oxford Delegacy of Local Examinations 1997]

Data response question

This task is based on a question set by the University of Oxford Delegacy of Local Examinations in 1997. Read the piece below and study the table. In answering the questions that follow you should use not only the information given, but also your own knowledge of economics, economic analysis and economic institutions.

Changes in the nature of investment

One of the recent puzzles in economics relates to investment. It simply doesn't behave as it used to. For example, even though interest rates have been falling, investment expenditure seems to have remained fairly stable.

One possible explanation is that, because of the recent rapid technical advances in computers and electronics, the price of many investment goods has fallen sharply in real terms, and their productivity has increased. So now you can replace your plant more cheaply than before, and get increased productivity and capacity as well.

Several things flow from this. To start with, there is an implication that one of the important barriers to entry has been reduced, with consequential effects on market structures and the nature of competition. Secondly, there must be a shift away from labour towards capital, with implications for employment and unemployment, differential effects on wages and earnings by skill, possible differences between the sexes, and between regions.

Again, if investment is now relatively cheap and less responsive to interest rate changes, the government may have to rethink macroeconomic policy. The investment multiplier may not have changed, but the ability to boost investment has. The government may have to place more reliance on other forms of expenditure to kickstart the economy.

Table A Investment in the UK, 1986–95

Year	Gross fixed capital formation (£bn at 1990 prices)	Profits (£bn at 1990 prices)	Average earnings index (1990 = 100)	Gross national product (£bn at 1990 prices)	Employment index (1990 = 100)
1986	83.7	71.1	71.3	493.3	91.0
1987	92.3	84.5	76.8	515.9	93.1
1988	105.2	86.6	83.5	543.2	96.2
1989	114.5	83.7	91.2	552.6	99.1
1990	107.6	75.5	100.0	551.8	100.0
1991	97.4	64.7	108.0	539.7	96.7
1992	96.0	64.5	114.6	541.1	94.7
1993	96.5	76.2	118.5	551.3	93.4
1994	99.5	91.4	123.3	580.2	93.8
1995	100.7	97.5	127.4	591.8	94.7

Source: *Economic Trends and Financial Statistics*, CSO.

1. (a) The article states that even though interest rates have been falling, investment expenditure seems to have remained fairly stable. Is this the relationship economic theory would predict? [4 marks]
   (b) Using the data in Table A, assess the relative importance of other factors which influence investment. [12 marks]
2. (a) Use economic analysis to show how changes in the nature of investment could affect earnings and the size of employment referred to in the third paragraph. [12 marks]
   (b) To what extent is there evidence in the table to support your argument in (a)? [8 marks]
3. (a) Explain carefully how the changes in the nature of investment could give rise to the changes in market structure suggested at the beginning of the third paragraph. [8 marks]
   (b) Evaluate the potential effect of these changes for consumers. [14 marks]
4. Assess the extent and nature of any changes in government policy to stimulate the economy that may have to be considered, given the change in the nature of investment. [22 marks]

Chapter Two

Taxation

'The primary aim of tax policy is to raise sufficient revenue for government to pay for the services which its policies require, and to service its debt, while keeping the overall burden of tax as low as possible. … It is essential that tax policy is based on clear principles. These are to encourage work, savings and investment, and fairness.'
Financial Statement and Budget Report, HM Treasury, July 1997

The tax burden

More than 200 years ago, Benjamin Franklin observed that nothing in this world was more certain 'except death and taxes'. A modern version of this might be that nothing is more certain than that higher public spending means, ultimately, higher taxation.

Governments, even those determined to cut public spending and reduce taxation, have found it difficult to do so. Public spending has tended to rise as a proportion of GDP, as we shall see in Chapter 3, and this has meant a rising **tax burden**.

Although opinion polls regularly show that majority public opinion would accept higher taxation to fund, for example, additional education and health spending, governments that raise taxes tend to be unpopular. Starting with Margaret Thatcher's election victory in 1979, the Conservative party's strongest card was its pledge to reduce taxation. This continued until the 1992 election when, under John Major, the party's election manifesto said: 'A lightly taxed economy generates more economic growth, and more revenue. High taxes kill the goose that lays the golden eggs.' Unfortunately for the Conservatives, the next two years saw the biggest tax rises in Britain's peacetime history, as the government attempted to reduce a budget deficit swelled by recession – which reduces the growth of tax revenues – and rapid growth in public spending. The Conservatives lost their reputation as a low-tax party.

There was still widespread mistrust of the Labour party, however. One of the reasons for the party's defeat in the 1992 general election had been its tax plans, in particular an intention to increase income tax rates for the better off. Although only a minority of people pay the top rate of income tax, currently 40 per cent, many more people aspire to being well enough off to do so.

Thus, prior to the 1997 general election, Gordon Brown, as shadow chancellor, pledged not to increase either the basic (23 per cent) or top (40 per cent) rate of income tax or to increase value-added tax (17.5 per cent). He also promised that, when circumstances permitted, a Labour government would introduce a reduced rate of income tax of 10 per cent on the first slice of taxable income. This was introduced in 1999 on the first £1500 of taxable income. Under the Conservatives this reduced rate was 20 per cent.

The dilemma, however, remains. How is it possible to meet growing demand for higher public expenditure and at the same time reduce, or at least not increase, taxation, in order to reward hard work, responsibility and success through the tax system?

Taxes are set to rise, admits Blair

GEORGE JONES

Taxation will rise over the lifetime of this parliament, Tony Blair admitted in the Commons yesterday. With Gordon Brown unveiling his third budget on Tuesday, the Tories claimed it was the first time that Mr Blair had acknowledged the government was putting up taxes by 'stealth'.

Labour came to power promising not to raise the basic or top rate of income tax and has so far stuck to this pledge. But the Tories claim that the Chancellor is raising an extra £40 billion over this parliament by increasing other taxes.

At question time in the Commons, William Hague, the Tory leader, challenged Mr Blair over calculations by the Confederation of British Industry that business taxes had increased by £5 billion as a result of the last two budgets. He said that business and the public had been forced to endure rises in petrol duty and stamp duty among other 'stealth tax rises'.

The Prime Minister replied that the *tax burden* 'will rise over this parliament' while maintaining that the increase would be 'at or below' the level predicted by the Conservatives in their last budget.

The Tories said that figures supplied by the Commons library showed that the tax burden would rise from 35.7 per cent of national wealth in 1996–97, the last year the Tories were in power, to 37.7 per cent in 2001–2. Francis Maude, the Tory Treasury spokesman, said 'At long last, Tony Blair has been forced to admit that taxes are going up by stealth under Labour.'

Daily Telegraph, 4 March 1999

Direct and indirect taxation

Direct taxation refers to those taxes levied mainly on income. Individuals pay income tax and National Insurance Contributions (NICs) on their earnings. Companies pay corporation tax on profits.

Indirect taxation is levied, not on income, but on spending. Value-added tax (VAT) is one indirect tax, others include the excise duties on petrol, alcohol and tobacco.

Direct taxes are usually **progressive** in that the higher an individual's earnings, or the greater a company's profits, the more tax is paid. Above a certain threshold of income, for example, people pay a higher rate of income tax, currently 40 per cent. Indirect taxation is less progressive, and can be **regressive** – a poor person buying a packet of cigarettes pays the same tax as a rich person. Governments have, however, tried to introduce a progressive element into indirect taxation. Food, children's clothing and other necessities are zero-rated for VAT purposes, while household gas and electricity carries a 5 per cent rate, in comparison with the normal 17.5 per cent rate. These necessities make up a larger proportion of the spending of low-income households.

A perfectly **proportionate** tax system would be one in which people paid the same proportion in taxation, whatever their income level.

Hypothecated taxes are raised for a specific purpose. A tax on road-users used only on building of new roads would be a hypothecated tax.

The principles of taxation

More than 200 years after the publication of *The Wealth of Nations* (1776), Adam Smith's four 'canons' of taxation continue to form the basis of modern tax systems. They are:

- taxes should be based on the ability to pay
- taxes should be easy and cheap to collect
- the method of paying taxes should be convenient for taxpayers
- there should be certainty in the system, with taxpayers knowing how much they need to pay, and when.

Later economists have also stressed the need for taxes to be flexible – capable of being altered to meet new circumstances.

Taxation, incentives and the supply side

Legend has it that the supply-side revolution began in the USA in the 1970s when Professor Arthur Laffer drew his famous **Laffer curve** on a napkin for a journalist from the *Wall Street Journal*. As Figure 4 demonstrates, it showed that, beyond a certain level, higher tax rates will produce a diminishing amount of government revenue, because people have a disincentive to work, and because they, and their accountants, have an incentive to seek out ways of avoiding tax.

In the 1980s in Britain such considerations were a prime factor in reductions in the top marginal rate of income tax from 83 to 40 per cent, and in the basic rate from 33 to 25 (later 23) per cent.

In fact the evidence, both theoretical and empirical, for such incentive effects is thin. It comes down to a basic question: When tax rates fall do people work harder, because they keep a greater share of their income? Or do they work less hard, because by working fewer hours they can keep the same level of after-tax income.

Attempts to study this puzzle empirically have mostly concluded that the majority of people do not have the ability to vary their working hours (or their salary does not vary according to the hours they work). For those who can vary their hours, such as owner-managers, separating lower tax rates from other factors has proved difficult. The theoretical argument is as follows.

Consider Figure 5. 'Indifference curve' I reflects those combinations of income and hours of leisure about which the individual is indifferent – he or she cannot choose between them. To accept fewer hours of leisure, the person would require an ever-increasing amount of income to compensate, and vice versa. The individual's chosen combination of work and leisure is reached when indifference curve I just touches the sloping budget line, which joins the Y and L axes. He or she chooses L hours of leisure (the remainder being working time) for an income level Y.

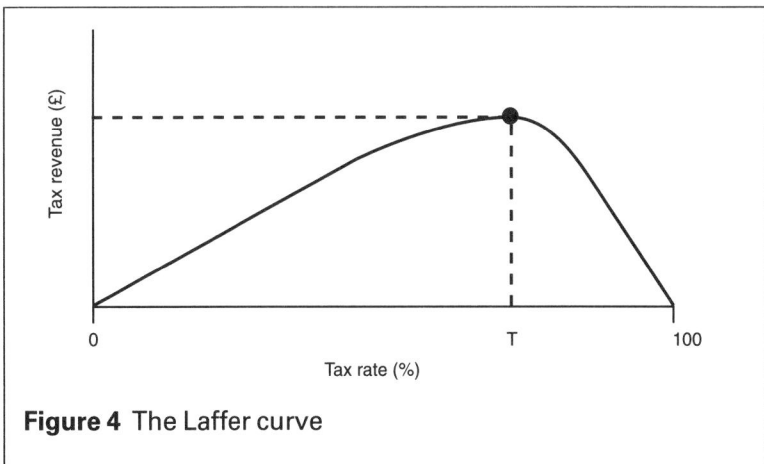

Figure 4 The Laffer curve

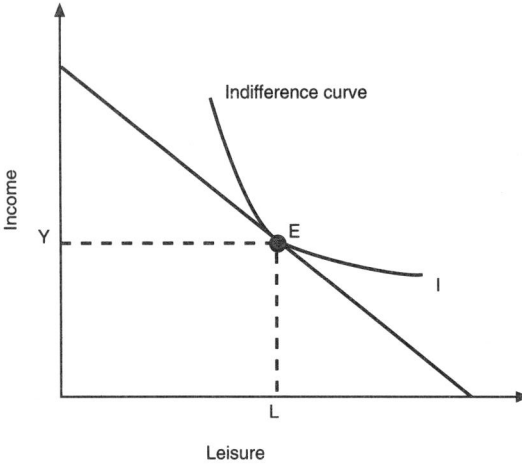

Figure 5 The work/leisure trade-off

One possible effect of reductions in tax rates is shown in Figure 6. Lower tax rates have the effect of steepening the budget line – for every hour worked (and thus for every hour of leisure foregone) the amount of after-tax income is greater than before. In this example, the new

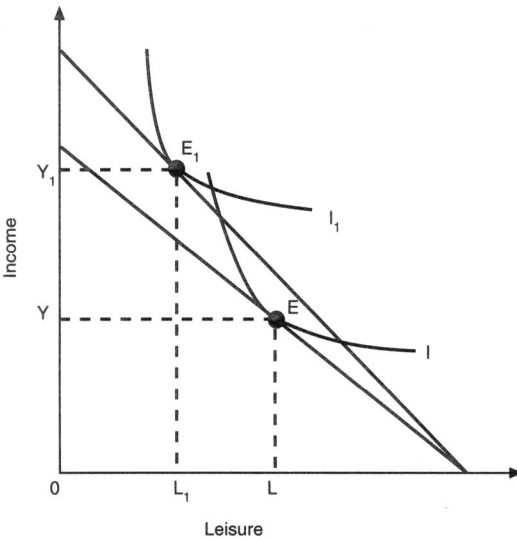

Figure 6 Tax cuts and the work/leisure trade-off

indifference curve which touches the budget line is I_1, and this generates a smaller amount of leisure hours (L_1 instead of L) – and thus a greater amount of hours worked – for a higher income, Y_1 instead of Y. Lower tax rates have thus produced positive incentive effects – longer hours are worked. This is not, however, the only possibility.

Consider now Figure 7, which shows an alternative possibility. If the indifference curve which touches the budget line is I_2, then the effect of a cut in taxes is to produce an increase in the amount of leisure hours from L to L_2, and therefore a reduction in hours worked. In this example, the individual gets the best of both worlds. He or she ends up with a slightly higher income, Y_2, than before but for a smaller number of hours worked.

So which is it more likely to be? There are two distinct effects from a tax cut – the **substitution effect** and the **income effect**. The cut in tax rates has made each hour worked more valuable to the individual, and thus increased the opportunity cost of leisure time. This substitution effect should encourage people to substitute hours of work for hours of leisure, as was the case in Figure 6. Pulling against this, however, is the income effect, in which the individual can work fewer hours for the same, or even for a higher income, than before. Leisure is a 'normal good', demand for which increases as income rises.

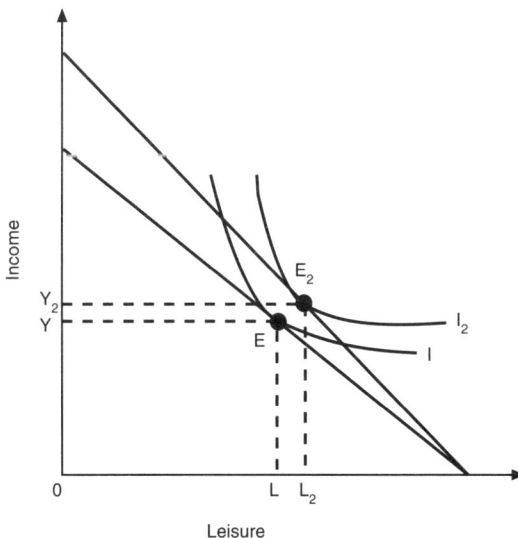

Figure 7 Tax cuts and a reduction in hours worked

Which of these two effects will dominate, and therefore whether or not people will work harder or take it easier, will depend on individual circumstances and preferences.

Taxation and the distribution of income

While the primary purpose of taxation is for governments to raise the

---

Tackling poverty and extending opportunity

A major Treasury study on the causes and scale of poverty and inequality in Britain and the best means of tackling it was launched today by Chancellor Gordon Brown, Social Security Secretary Alistair Darling and Minister for Public Health Tessa Jowell.

The six-month research study, *Tackling Poverty and Extending Opportunity*, contains shocking conclusions on the scale of poverty and inequality, and the passage of inequality from generation to generation.

The study, based on 1997 figures, shows that 12 million people in the UK – nearly a quarter of the population – live in *relative poverty*. That is almost three times the number in 1979. Inequality rose by a third between 1977 and 1996 – almost unique among developed countries. Inequality is passed from generation to generation, so the children of the low-paid are much more likely to be low-paid.

It is the most extensive government analysis yet of child poverty, showing that four million children were living in poverty in 1995 – three times the number of 20 years ago. Two out of every five children are born poor. Many of them are born to families who were not poor before the birth of their child. As many as one in six families are pushed into poverty with the birth of a child; poverty damages a child's life chances. By the time children are 22 months old there are clear social class differences in their rate of *educational development*, and these differences continue to widen when children start school.

The study concludes that work and access to work is the key driver in Britain today, and lack of work is the primary cause of poverty. It shows that the number of *workless households* has more than doubled over the last 20 years. Work is the best route out of poverty: 80 per cent of people who moved into work moved out of the poorest fifth. Education is key to success in the labour market: what you learn is directly related to what you earn (half of people who have no qualifications are without a job).

Work history also has a profound effect on life chances of individuals and their children: in the mid-1990s half of those leaving unemployment were unemployed again within the year; people get stuck in a low-pay, no-pay cycle. The number of men stuck in this cycle or in a long-term, low-paid job has doubled since the early 1980s, from one in 14 to one in seven.

Source: HM Treasury, 29 March 1999

---

revenues needed to finance public spending, an important secondary objective, in modern times, has been the *redistribution of income*.

In the 1970s, when Labour was previously in power, not only was the overall tax burden higher as a percentage of GDP, but the tax system was heavily progressive. The basic rate of income tax was 33 per cent but the highest marginal rate was 83 per cent. Above a certain level of income, in other words, people would keep only 17 pence from every extra pound they earned.

This changed significantly under the Conservative government elected in 1979. The basic rate of income tax was cut to 30 per cent, and the top rate to 60 per cent, financed by an increase in VAT from 8 per cent and 12.5 per cent to a uniform rate of 15 per cent. The tax system was thus made more regressive at a stroke. The Conservatives persisted with this strategy, eventually reducing the top rate of income tax to 40 per cent and the basic rate to 23 per cent, while raising VAT further, to 17.5 per cent. The period of Conservative rule, and particularly the 1980s, saw a sharp rise in income inequality in Britain.

The dilemma for the Labour party in the run-up to the May 1997 general election was that, while many of its supporters favoured using the tax system to take money away from 'fat cats' and redistribute it to people on low incomes, the party leadership feared an adverse response from voters towards any plan for raising income tax rates. Thus, Labour went into the election pledging not to increase income tax rates or VAT.

In practice the Blair government has tried to redistribute income in other ways, by taxing share dividends more heavily, and by introducing a new tax 'credit' – the working families' tax credit – designed to help people on lower incomes. It has also concentrated its tax-cutting agenda on a new lower starting rate of income tax, of 10 per cent.

Other tax changes have, however, been unfavourable to those on low incomes – for example the decision to raise the excise duties on petrol by 6 per cent a year in real terms, with a similar increase for cigarette duties. Both impact disproportionately on lower-income households.

Tax policy in practice: the budget

The budget, which is presented in March, sets out the government's tax plans for the coming fiscal year beginning in April. Prior to that, each November, the chancellor publishes a pre-budget report, or 'green' budget (as in Green Paper) which sets out tax options for the following spring.

Under the Conservatives from 1993 to 1997, there was a 'unified' November budget, setting out both tax and public expenditure plans. The Labour government decided, however, to set three-year spending

Table 2 Government receipts in 1998/99 (£ billion)

Inland Revenue	
Income tax	85.5
Corporation tax	29.8
Windfall tax	2.6
Petroleum revenue tax	0.5
Capital gains tax	2.4
Inheritance tax	1.8
Stamp duties	4.7
Customs & Excise	
Value-added tax	51.7
Fuel duties	21.5
Tobacco duties	8.3
Alcohol duties	5.9
Others	5.8
Social security contributions and others	
Social security contributions	54.9
Business rates	15.2
Council tax	11.8
Vehicle excise duties	4.6
Others	7.7
Total (tax and social security)	315.2

Source: Financial Statement and Budget Report, HM Treasury, March 1999

plans for government departments, so the annual budget is now concerned with taxation.

Some changes occur automatically at budget time. Examples are the 'indexation' (increasing in line with inflation) of most tax allowances and some excise duties, such as on alcohol. Other decisions are known as **discretionary tax changes,** when the Chancellor raises or lowers taxes to meet the government's objectives. Table 2 shows the main sources of government tax revenues.

Tax harmonization in Europe
An important issue both now and in the future is the **harmonization** of taxes within Europe.

When the Labour government took power in May 1997 it pledged to remove value-added tax on domestic fuel and power (gas and electricity bills), introduced by the previous Conservative government. However, it was soon discovered that, under EU rules, VAT on fuel could not be removed entirely but only reduced, to 5 per cent. This is because VAT rates have been harmonized in Europe. Why is this?

Imagine two neighbouring countries, with no trade barriers or restrictions on the movement of people between them. One has a VAT rate of 5 per cent on goods, the other sets a rate of 20 per cent. People from the high-VAT country would cross the border to buy all their goods in the low-VAT country. The former would lose tax revenue and its economy would suffer. The latter would gain on both counts.

Thus in 1992, ahead of the start of the European 'single market' at the end of that year, finance ministers in Europe agreed on a minimum standard rate of VAT of 15 per cent (fuel, food and other essentials can be taxed at a lower rate but again within preset limits). The new minimum rate of VAT did not eliminate all variations – VAT rates currently range from 15 per cent in Luxembourg to 25 per cent in Sweden and Denmark – but it reduced them. The experience of the USA, where individual states operate different rates of sales tax, suggests that a single market does not require complete harmonization of taxes.

Pressure for greater harmonization of other taxes – on investment, on companies, and even on income – has been quite strong within Europe. It is argued, for example, that countries offering lower rates of corporation tax are providing an unfair incentive for companies to locate there. Similarly, countries offering lower income tax rates, particularly for higher earners, can be said to be offering a powerful incentive to managers to locate their businesses there.

Harmonization of taxes can be expected to increase in Europe. The Chancellor has faced pressure from the tobacco and drinks industries to reduce the excise duties on cigarettes and alcohol, because of the loss of business to the so-called 'Calais run', where people can buy cheaper in northern France, where duty levels are far lower.

Perfect harmonization of taxes is, however, unlikely. Some countries in Europe raise much more tax as a percentage of GDP than do others. Portugal, for example, raises only 33 per cent of its GDP in tax, compared with 50 per cent in several other EU countries.

KEY WORDS

Tax burden	Laffer curve
Direct taxation	Substitution effect
Indirect taxation	Income effect
Progressive	Indexation
Regressive	Discretionary tax changes
Proportionate	Harmonization
Hypothecated taxes	

Reading list

Atkinson, B., Livesey, F. and Milward, R., Chapter 20 in *Applied Economics*, Macmillan, 1998.

Grant, S., Chapters 31 and 33 in *Stanlake's Introductory Economics*, 7th edn, Longman, 1999.

Healey, N. and Cook, M., Chapter 6 in *Supply Side Economics*, 3rd edn, Heinemann Educational, 1996.

Sloman, J., Chapter 17 in *Economics*, 3rd edn, Prentice Hall, 1997.

Useful website

Institute for Fiscal Studies: www.ifs.org.uk/

Essay topics

1. Whenever governments increase personal income taxes, people protest.

   (a) Consider why taxes are necessary. [10 marks]

   (b) Compare the likely effects of an increase in personal income tax with an increase in a tax on company profits. [15 marks] [University of Cambridge Local Examinations Syndicate 1997]

2. Assess the arguments for and against shifting the burden of taxation from direct to indirect taxes. [25 marks]

Data response question

This task is based on a question set by the University of Cambridge Local Examinations Syndicate in 1996. Study the data below relating to the burden of taxation, and then answer the questions that follow.

The changing burden of taxation

In the UK there has been a clear and deliberate change of emphasis in the burden of taxation. In particular, direct tax rates have fallen; but at the same time, higher-income earners have continued to contribute the biggest share of total income tax receipts. Table A shows how the UK compares with three other countries in terms of the burden of income tax, for a married man with two children in 1992/93.

Table A Income tax and social security payments as a
percentage of income (married man with two children), 1992/93

	Income level			
	£20 000	£35 000	£50 000	£100 000
UK	26.1	28.5	32.0	36.0
Germany	29.7	30.9	31.5	39.1
France	17.8	23.8	27.7	37.9
USA (New York)	20.2	26.9	31.0	36.8

Source: Coopers & Lybrand, Deloitte

Figure A Percentage of total income going in income tax and
social security payments

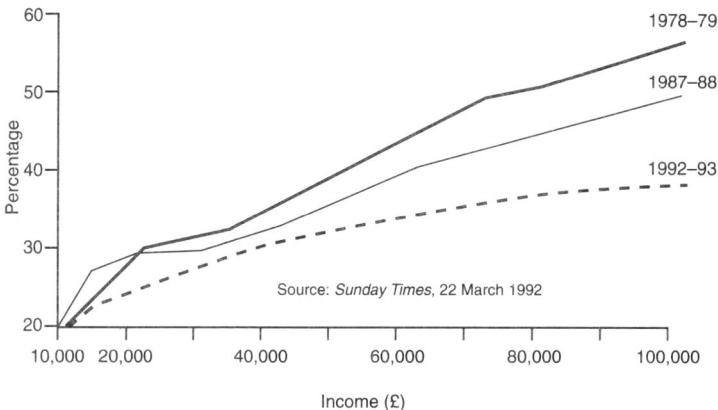

1. (a) From Table A, which country appeared to have the greatest
   burden of direct tax at a gross income of £100 000? Explain your
   answer. [2 marks]
   (b) Compare the net income, after income tax and social security
   payments have been deducted, of a family in the UK and a family in
   France earning a gross annual income of: (i) £20 000, (ii) £100 000.
   [2 marks]
   (c) Which country had the most progressive system of taxes on
   incomes? Explain your answer. [2 marks]
   (d) With reference to the countries given, explain why additional
   information is required to assess the total burden of taxation in a
   particular country. [4 marks]

2. (a) From the tax changes made in the period shown in Figure A, which income earners in the UK apparently gained (i) most, and (ii) least? Explain your answers. [4 marks]

(b) Evaluate the advantages and disadvantages of reducing the average rates of direct taxation. [6 marks]

Chapter Three

Public expenditure and the changing role of fiscal policy

'Sound finance may be right psychologically, but economically it is a depressing influence.'
John Maynard Keynes

'The government's two strict fiscal rules define how sound public finances are to be delivered:

- *the Golden Rule – on average over the economic cycle, the government will borrow only to invest and not to fund current spending; and*
- *the Sustainable Investment Rule – net public debt as a proportion of GDP will be held over the economic cycle at a stable and prudent level.*

The framework is based on achieving sound public finances and long-term economic stability.'
Pre-budget Report, HM Treasury, November 1998

Fiscal policy and the growth of public spending

Fiscal means 'pertaining to public revenue' – in other words taxation. Fiscal **policy,** however, refers to both sides of government accounts, revenue and expenditure. The growth of public expenditure throughout much of the twentieth century ensured an enhanced role for fiscal policy. This growth has occurred in stages.

• Victorian values

In the early years of the century, taxation and public spending were equivalent to roughly 10 per cent of gross domestic product (GDP) and governments typically ran a **budget surplus** because tax revenues exceeded public spending. Throughout the Victorian and early Edwardian era, governments aimed to repay some of the **national debt.**

• Keynes and the Great Depression

The First World War (1914–18) increased the national debt and was followed by substantially higher public expenditure. This was due not only to the early stages of the modern **welfare state,** but also to the influence of John Maynard Keynes, who argued for higher government spending as a solution to the Great Depression. Public spending was typically 20 per cent of GDP or more in the inter-war years.

● The modern welfare state

During the Second World War (1939–45) the government had taken a much bigger role in the economy. This was continued by the 1945–51 Labour administration led by Attlee. The modern welfare state, based on the **Beveridge Report** of 1942, came into being. The National Health Service (NHS) was created in 1948. More than 20 per cent of industry was taken into public ownership, including coal, rail, road freight, civil aviation, gas, electricity, iron and steel. The government accepted the prescriptions of Keynes, committing itself to full employment, and state intervention to achieve that end.

The direct influence of government increased. From 30–40 per cent of GDP in the 1950s and 60s, government spending rose to the equivalent of 40–50 per cent of GDP in the period from the 1970s to the 90s, even under Margaret Thatcher's Conservative government, which was committed to 'rolling back the frontiers of the state'.

During the 1990s, however, public spending was brought back under control. Some economists predict that increasing demand for public services and the pressures of an ageing population will lead to an inevitable rise in spending as a proportion of GDP. Figure 8 shows the post-war record.

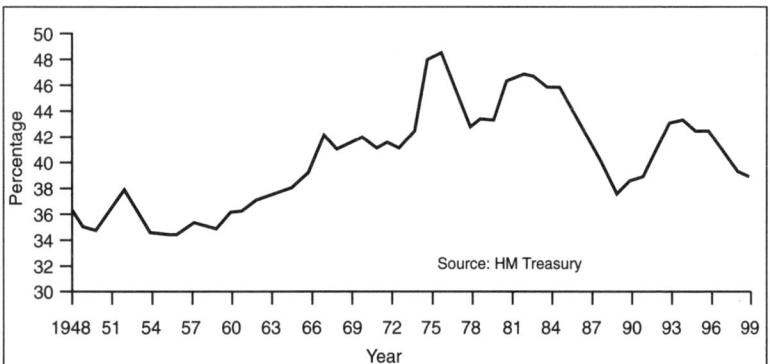

Figure 8 General government expenditure as a percentage of GDP

Spending and transfers

In considering the level of public expenditure, it is necessary to distinguish between direct spending by government, for example on the police, the armed forces, or road-building, and **transfers**.

Brown's economic gamble could easily go awry

JOHN JAY

The days of rolling back the frontiers of the state are over – that much is clear from Gordon Brown's comprehensive spending review unveiled last week. Government spending as a percentage of gross domestic product will rise for the next few years of Labour administration. Instead of the state deploying some of the dividends of growth on cutting taxes and/or repaying government debt, Tony Blair's new Labour will spend everything on public services. Money that could sensibly be left in private hands to be used creatively to generate wealth and jobs will instead be soaked up by the state.

Brown is therefore gambling with fiscal policy. If growth slows and unemployment starts to rise – 2 per cent growth is typically needed to keep employment stable because of productivity advances stemming from technological innovation – the social-security bill will soar and either the public deficit will rise or taxes will have to go up. Spending and tax yields are hugely sensitive to changes in the economy – and Brown's sums could easily go badly wrong.

The Chancellor is also showing a touching faith in the idea that he can pump vast sums into the spending departments without it leaking away in excessive pay awards and that investment in the public sector can yield returns without the introduction of private-sector disciplines. He will wave his big Treasury stick if spending ministers are wasteful, withholding cash if necessary. But what is really needed in so many government departments is not the threat from Big Brother but the fresh incentives that can be provided through competitive tendering and contracting out. The Tories did a lot but there is a long way to go.

Sunday Times, 19 July 1998

Transfers, such as pensions, the jobseekers' allowance and other social security benefits, do not represent direct spending by government. Instead, they represent a transfer from one set of people – taxpayers – to another set, claimants.

Many taxpayers, indeed, also receive benefits. Pensioners with a private pension as well as the basic state pension are taxpayers. So too are taxpaying households who receive, say, child benefit.

Economists distinguish between direct government spending and transfers. The former is a direct claim by government on the nation's resources and is 30 per cent of the UK's GDP. The latter is a form of redistribution but, once the transfer has been made, the government has no control over the way the money is spent.

In practical terms the level of transfers is important because it affects the level of taxation. The rising share of taxation as a proportion of GDP in modern times has largely been due to rising social security payments. Governments wishing to hold down taxation therefore need to control social security payments. To the extent that such payments rise, for example, when unemployment goes up, this is difficult. There is, however, certain action the government can take. Soon after being elected in 1979, the Thatcher government linked the annual uprating of state pensions and other social security benefits to prices (the retail prices index) rather than to earnings, which tend to rise faster. By the 1990s, this measure was saving several billion pounds a year.

In March 1999, the Chancellor announced that a minimum income guarantee for pensioners would rise in line with earnings rather than prices.

Debts and deficits

The *national debt* is the amount of borrowing that the government has accumulated over time. There are two ways of measuring this debt.

- Net public sector debt stood at £349 billion, or 40 per cent of GDP in 1999.
- General government gross debt, which is used for the purposes of the Maastricht conditions for European economic and monetary union, was £409 billion, or 48 per cent of GDP. Under the Maastricht treaty it was required to be 60 per cent of GDP or below.

The difference between these two figures for debt is that the former is reduced by the amount of the government's short-term financial assets, such as bank deposits and foreign currency reserves.

The *budget deficit* (or surplus) is the difference between government spending and tax receipts in any one year. There are several ways of measuring the budget deficit or surplus.

For many years the **public sector borrowing requirement** (PSBR) was the most commonly used measure. More recently, this has been renamed the **public sector net cash requirement** (PSNCR). The government currently stresses other measures, notably **net borrowing** and the **current budget surplus/deficit**. It is not necessary to concern ourselves with the precise detail of these definitions.

When governments run a budget deficit, or borrow, fiscal policy is expansionary; and vice versa when governments run a surplus, or repay debt. There is, however, one important proviso. This is that budget deficits are a normal consequence of economic downturns – tax revenues decline and public spending on unemployment benefits increases – while the budget will tend towards a surplus when economic growth is strong. Economists sometimes call these effects the **automatic stabilizers**. It is important in judging whether economic policy is expansionary or contractionary to assess the position of the economy in the economic cycle.

Deficits and 'crowding out'

Why do governments need to control budget deficits? One reason, which the government cited during the 1980s when monetarism was in vogue, was that government borrowing added to the growth of the money supply and was therefore considered to be inflationary. A more traditional reason is that borrowing by governments now means that future generations will be left with the burden of repaying that debt – there is an **inter-generational transfer** of the tax burden. Future generations will have to pay higher taxes to fund public spending now.

A third reason is called **financial crowding out**. The more that the government borrows by issuing UK government bonds (called 'gilts' because the certificates used to have a gilt-edged border), the more – given a limited supply of funds – interest rates will be forced higher, discouraging private sector firms from borrowing to invest. The public sector is thus crowding out the private sector. In the late 1990s, thanks to low levels of government borrowing and low inflation, long-term interest rates on UK gilts fell to their lowest level for more than 30 years. Thus, the public sector was leaving room for the private sector to borrow and invest.

Keynesians, it should be said, dispute this. They argue that 'crowding in' is a more powerful effect. When the government invests, they argue, this gives the business world the confidence to do so as well.

The composition of public spending

The composition of public spending has changed significantly in the post-war period. In 1950, in the wake of the Second World War, the biggest programme was defence (with a budget equivalent to 6.6 per cent of GDP), followed by social security (5.1 per cent), health (3.6 per cent), education (3.4 per cent) and housing (2.6 per cent).

Fifty years on, the four biggest programmes remain the same, although their order has changed significantly, with social security easily having the biggest budget (12.4 per cent of GDP), followed by health and personal social services (6.7 per cent), education (4.6 per cent) and defence (2.7 per cent).

Government spending on housing has declined sharply, because of the rise in owner-occupation and the sale of a large part of the council housing stock to the public under the right-to-buy legislation. Figure 9 summarizes the recent position.

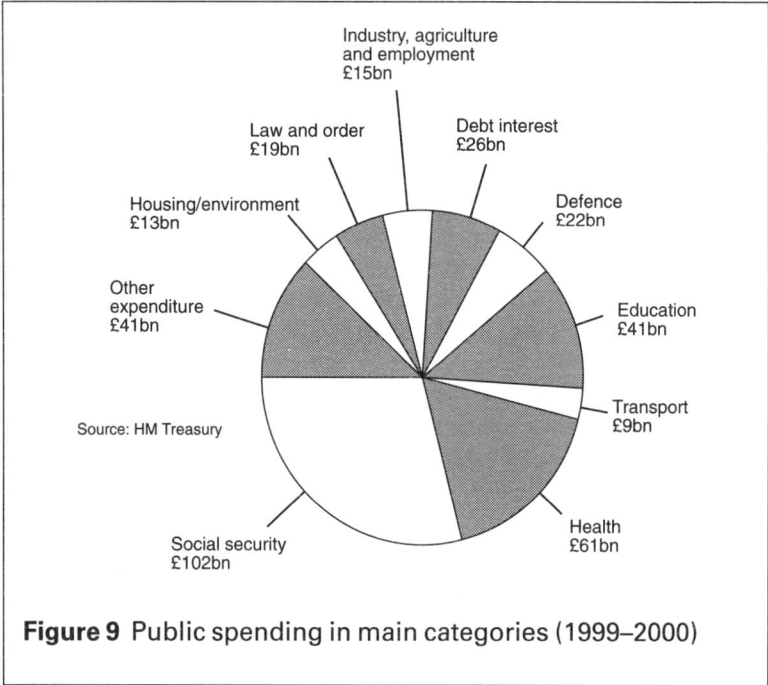

Industry, agriculture and employment £15bn

Law and order £19bn

Debt interest £26bn

Housing/environment £13bn

Defence £22bn

Other expenditure £41bn

Education £41bn

Source: HM Treasury

Transport £9bn

Social security £102bn

Health £61bn

Figure 9 Public spending in main categories (1999–2000)

The comprehensive spending review

One significant change introduced by the Labour government elected in 1997 was to conduct a **comprehensive spending review**. This was to ensure that spending was being directed to the areas the government considered were its main priorities.

Also, and significantly, spending limits were to be agreed for all government departments for a three-year period, both to provide individual departments with greater certainty for planning purposes, and to prevent the normal sharp pre-election rise in government outlays. Economists have long observed that public spending tends to rise, and tax rates fall, in the run-up to general elections.

The main outcomes of the review, announced in July 1998, were:

- a 5.1 per cent annual real rise in education spending, equivalent to £19 billion extra over three years, raising the share of education spending to 5 per cent of GDP by 2001–02
- a 4.7 per cent annual rise in NHS spending, equivalent to more than £20 billion extra over three years
- a 1.8 per cent real rise in other government programmes
- an increase in public sector net investment from £6.7 billion to £13 billion.

Within an annual real rise in government spending of 2.75 per cent a year, the government's priorities were thus education (one aim being to reduce class sizes for 5–7 year-olds), health (cutting hospital waiting lists) and public investment. Other measures were aimed at improving the efficiency of the public sector, to ensure taxpayers received value for money.

A new political consensus on public spending?

Before the 1997 general election, many Conservative politicians favoured reducing public spending as a share of GDP.

It was argued that in very prosperous economies in the world, such as the USA, public spending was only around 30 per cent of GDP compared with 40 per cent in the UK and 50 per cent in many other European countries. The argument was that lower levels of public spending permit lower taxation, and that this provides individuals and businesses with greater 'supply-side' incentives, as discussed in the previous chapter.

Many Conservatives also argued that, such were the likely future pressures on the NHS and social security spending as a result of an ageing population – older people require more healthcare spending and the amount that would have to be paid out in state pensions would increase – it would be necessary to find private-sector ways of funding long-term care for the elderly, and of encouraging a higher proportion of people to take out private pensions. The Conservatives were also keen to encourage private education.

This party policy changed in 1999 when Peter Lilley, in a speech as deputy leader of the Conservative party, said there was only a limited role for the private sector in providing for these various aspects of the welfare state (health, education and social security) and that a future Conservative government would recognize this. Francis Maude, the shadow chancellor, also pledged that a Conservative government would match the spending increases on health and education by the Labour government.

Although Conservatives denied that this represented a policy reversal, or an abandonment of Thatcherism, it appeared to signal the end of the debate over the proper size of the state. In future, it appeared, both main parties would accept a public spending level of about 40 per cent of GDP.

Privatization

If you asked an international audience what was the most notable economic policy to have come out of Britain in the past 20 years or so, they would probably say **privatization**. Privatization, nowadays less frequently known as denationalization or **asset sales,** means in its most straightforward form precisely that – the sale of state assets to the private sector.

Between 1979 and 1997, Conservative governments sold 46 previously state-owned companies to the private sector (accounting for 900 000 jobs), including British Telecom, British Gas, the water, electricity and railway industries, British Airways, BAA (formerly the British Airports Authority), British Steel and Girobank.

It is difficult to overstate the scale of this change. It reflects a shift in philosophy from a belief that utilities providing the basics of life – water, electricity, gas, public transport – should be monopoly state suppliers, to a belief that these things are better run by the private sector. It was also lucrative for the government – asset sales raised nearly £70 billion between 1979 and 1997, although subsequently the government was accused of selling them off too cheaply.

Privatization can also, however, be widened to include other policy actions which allow the private sector into areas that were previously the exclusive domain of the state.

● Deregulation

Deregulation is the removal of legal and other barriers to entry into industries previously dominated by public provision. Bus deregulation allowed private operators into a market in which state or council-run services had dominated.

● Franchising

Franchising is the opening up of services previously provided 'in-house' by the public sector, through **compulsory competitive tendering.** Councils were required to allow private companies to tender for services they previously operated themselves, such as refuse collection.

● The private finance initiative

The **private finance initiative** (PFI), or public/private partnerships, arise when the public sector purchases services from a private sector partner. The private partner has generally undertaken the capital investment, for example the building of a new hospital or road, and the public sector pays for the use of that facility.

The value of the PFI for the government is that investment occurs which would previously have been constrained by the state of the public finances – tax or borrowing would have had to rise to fund the investment. The government set a target of more than £11 billion for PFI investment over the three-year period from 1998/99.

The case for and against privatization

In examining the case for privatization, it is worth recalling first why some activities were thought to be best performed by the state, or by state-owned corporations.

Arguments in favour of state control

The arguments in favour of state control were as follows:

- There are **natural monopolies** such as gas, electricity, water and the railways, where unit costs decline with increased output, and where competition would mean wasteful duplication of services. Allowing a private firm to run such natural monopolies would mean they benefited from excess monopoly profits.
- Where firms are state-owned, it is easier to deal directly with **externalities**, such as pollution from power stations.
- Certain large **high-risk projects**, which are indivisible (they cannot be broken up into smaller amounts of investment) would be difficult to finance privately. If you want to create a national electricity grid, for example, it is easier to spread the cost across all taxpayers.
- Nationalized industries, it was thought, would have better **industrial relations**, because workers would be less willing to take industrial action against organizations that they, as taxpayers, ultimately owned. For similar reasons it was thought that **productivity** (output per worker) would be higher in state-owned industries.
- State-owned industries could be used in support of government macroeconomic policy, by maintaining or increasing employment during times of recession.
- Nationalized industries could pursue investment and other strategies in the long-term interests of the country, whereas private firms were subject to pressures for short-term profit maximization – and could be punished by going out of business if they failed to provide what customers wanted.

Many of these arguments proved to be mistaken in practice. The industrial relations climate in nationalized industries was worse than in the private sector, because workers believed that such was the strategic importance of their industries and so large the public purse, strike action would normally bring rewards. Productivity was lower in the public sector, partly because of poor management. Investment, far from being easier to undertake, was subject to political constraints. The current private finance initiative is a recognition of the fact that, contrary to the theory, it is often easier for the private sector to finance large-scale 'public' investments.

Arguments in favour of privativation

There are several separate arguments in favour of privatization:

- *Incentives.* Private sector managers and directors have the carrot of being directly rewarded when profits improve.
- *Punishment.* Dismissal is the private sector penalty when things go badly. It is less likely to be the case within nationalized industries.
- *Political interference.* Decisions can be forced on nationalized industries by ministers for short-term political gain. The private sector has a freer hand.
- *Access to capital.* Private firms can raise funds for expansion from shareholders, whereas nationalized industries often come up against unrealistic Treasury targets for the rate of return on capital projects, or are constrained by public borrowing considerations from raising finance.

Privatization and regulation

One persistent criticism of privatization, as carried out by Conservative governments, is that it transferred monopolies from the public sector to the private sector, allowing excess profits to be made.

The response to this has been **regulation**, requiring the privatized utilities to maintain a specified level of service (including uneconomic aspects of the business) and controlling their prices. Within this the privatized utilities would then be free to achieve maximum profits.

Typically, under a formula devised by Professor Stephen Littlechild – who subsequently became the regulator for the electricity industry – privatized firms were required to set annual price rises on the basis of an **'RPI minus x'** formula. This meant that they could raise prices by no more than a specified amount (x) below the inflation rate (measured by the RPI, or retail prices index).

Thus, if inflation was 4.5 per cent, and x was 2 per cent, the maximum the industry would be able to raise prices was 2.5 per cent.

This formula was used by Oftel, the telecommunications regulator, set up on the privatization of BT in 1984, and by Ofgas, as gas regulator, and Offer, the electricity regulator. Ofwat, set up to regulate the privatized water industry, was the exception, setting an 'RPI *plus k*' formula. Water companies were allowed to raise their prices by *more* than inflation, by the maximum amount *k* per cent, on the understanding that the additional amount must be used to finance environmental improvements.

On taking office in 1997, the Labour government announced that it was reviewing the regulatory regime, with a view to consolidating the different regulatory bodies into a single large regulator.

The new Labour government also made clear its dissatisfaction with the way the regulatory process had been allowed to operate in the early years after privatization, allowing excess profits to be made. In the July 1997 budget it announced a £5 billion one-off **windfall tax** on the gas, electricity, water and telecommunications industries, to finance the New Deal for the long-term unemployed.

The approach to privatization can be seen to have changed as the policy matured. Initially, companies were sold as monopolies to the private sector, for example in the case of BT, and competition introduced only later. Later privatizations either reduced the period in which the privatized company was allowed to make monopoly profits or achieved the sale in a different way. Rail privatization, for example, did not sell British Rail in its entirety to a single private sector company, but split the sale into the track company, Railtrack, as well as rolling stock companies and a series of train operating companies, running different parts of the network. This did not prevent the charge of, in some cases, excess profit or, in many cases, of poor service.

The National Asset Register

Traditionally Labour governments were in favour of nationalization and Conservative governments went for denationalization, although it was not until after 1979 that privatization occurred on any scale.

By the time the Conservatives had privatized most of the big state-owned corporations, the Labour party's position was that it would not seek to renationalize them, because it would be too expensive to do so and there were other priorities for government spending. In practice, the Labour administration which took office in May 1997 has continued with sales of state assets, partly for the reason that this frees resources to be spent on other government provision.

After the general election the Treasury instructed all government departments to draw up a list of the assets they owned so that surplus assets such as buildings and land could be sold off. Thus was born the **National Asset Register**. A target has since been set for £22 billion of asset sales over the period 1998–2001.

KEY WORDS

Fiscal policy	Privatization
Budget surplus	Asset sales
National debt	Deregulation
Welfare state	Franchising
Beveridge Report	Compulsory competitive
Transfers	tendering
Public sector borrowing	Private finance initiative
requirement	Natural monopolies
Public sector net cash	Externalities
requirement	High-risk projects
Net borrowing	Industrial relations
Current budget surplus	Productivity
Automatic stabilizers	Regulation
Inter-generational transfer	RPI minus x
Financial crowding-out	Windfall tax
Comprehensive spending	National Asset Register
review	

Reading list

Atkinson, B., Livesey, F. and Milward, B., Chapter 19 in *Applied Economics*, Macmillan, 1998.

Bamford, C., Chapter 5 in *Transport Economics*, 2nd edn, Heinemann Educational, 1998.

Griffiths, A. and Wall, S. (eds), Chapters 15 and 16 in *Applied Economics*, 7th edn, Addison-Wesley Longman, 1997.

Hurl, B., *Privatization and the Public Sector*, 3rd edn, Heinemann Educational, 1995.

Useful website

HM Treasury: www.hm-treasury.gov.uk/

Essay topics

1. (a) Using examples to illustrate your answer, explain how the UK government uses fiscal economic policy to influence the ways in which resources are allocated between different uses. [12 marks]

(b) During the 1990s the UK government ran large budget deficits. Discuss whether the government should attempt to eliminate the PSBR and balance its budget. [13 marks] [Associated Examining Board 1998]

2. (a) Explain how the regulators (e.g. Ofwat and Oftel) in the UK have attempted to prevent the privatized utilities from abusing their monopoly power. [12 marks]

(b) Using examples to support your arguments, assess the strengths and weaknesses of the UK's approach to regulating privatized industries. [13 marks] [Associated Examining Board 1998]

Data response question

This task is based on a question set by the University of London Examinations and Assessment Council in 1996. First study all the charts below relating to tax receipts and government expenditure in the UK, and then aswer the questions that follow.

Figure A Public spending in the UK as a percentage of GDP

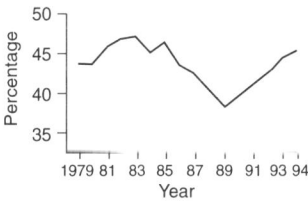

Figure B UK growth (annual percentage change in real GDP)

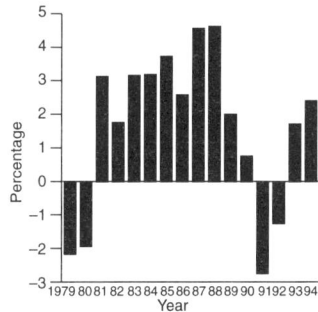

Figure C Public sector borrowing requirement, excluding privatization proceeds

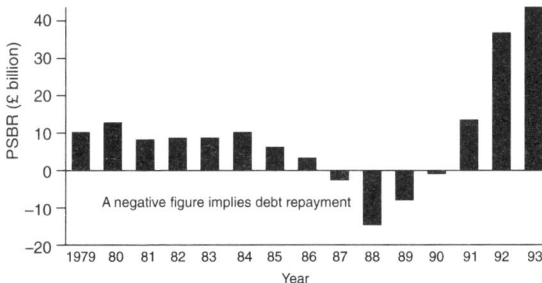

A negative figure implies debt repayment

Figure D Public expenditure, 1992/93

Total: £269 bn

Source: *The Economist*, 4 September 1993

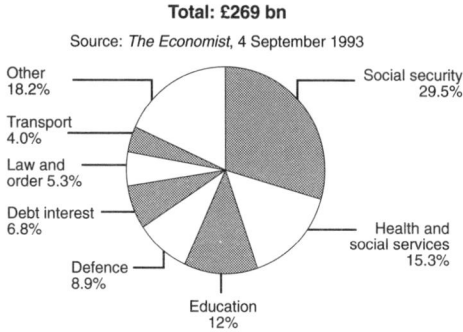

Other 18.2%
Transport 4.0%
Law and order 5.3%
Debt interest 6.8%
Defence 8.9%
Education 12%
Social security 29.5%
Health and social services 15.3%

Figure E Central government tax receipts

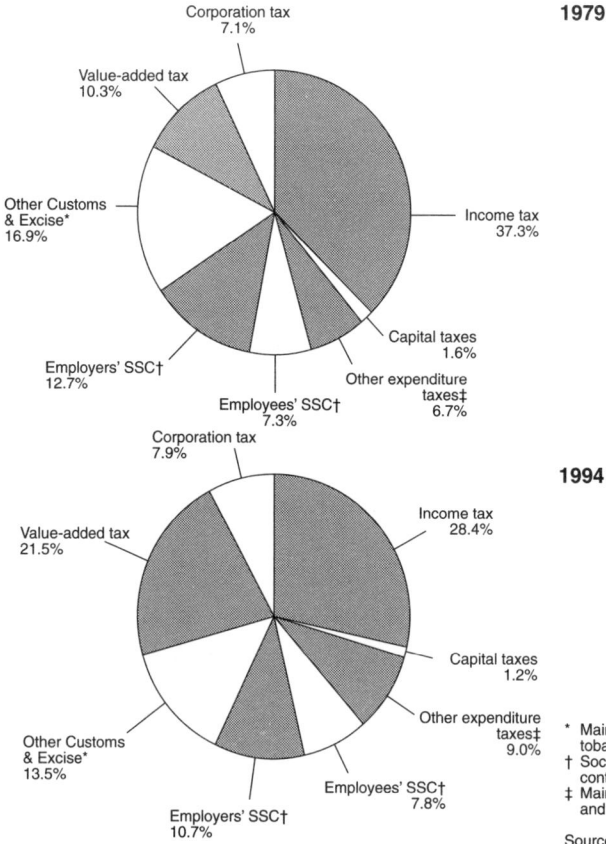

1979

Corporation tax 7.1%
Value-added tax 10.3%
Other Customs & Excise* 16.9%
Employers' SSC† 12.7%
Employees' SSC† 7.3%
Income tax 37.3%
Capital taxes 1.6%
Other expenditure taxes‡ 6.7%

1994

Corporation tax 7.9%
Value-added tax 21.5%
Other Customs & Excise* 13.5%
Employers' SSC† 10.7%
Employees' SSC† 7.8%
Income tax 28.4%
Capital taxes 1.2%
Other expenditure taxes‡ 9.0%

* Mainly duties on alcohol, tobacco and oil
† Social security contributions (SSC)
‡ Mainly business rates and road fund licence

Source: *Dataset*, 1995

1. Explain *one* factor which might account for the trend in public expenditure as a percentage of GDP since 1989. [3 marks]
2. (a) Why might you expect there to be a relationship between changes in real GDP and changes in the PSBR as a percentage of GDP [3 marks]
   (b) To what extent do the data in Figures B and C suggest that such a relationship existed between 1985 and 1993? [3 marks]
3. How does Figure D illustrate any *three* objectives of public expenditure? [6 marks]
4. Examine the likely economic effects of the changes in the relative importance of sources of government revenue on (i) incentives to work, and (ii) the distribution of income [6 + 4 marks]

Chapter Four

The Bank of England and monetary policy

'The Bank of England has been given operational independence to set interest rates to meet the government's inflation target – ensuring that interest rate decisions are taken on the basis of the long-term needs of the economy, not short-term political considerations.'
Pre-budget Report, HM Treasury, November 1998

What is monetary policy?

Monetary policy and fiscal policy represent the two most important levers for controlling the economy. As we have seen, fiscal policy refers to taxation and public spending. Monetary policy is concerned with setting **monetary conditions** in the economy.

This includes a range of connected factors, most importantly the level of **interest rates,** but also the **exchange rate,** and rates of growth of **money and credit.** In general, a policy of raising interest rates and, in a floating exchange rate regime, allowing the currency value to rise – a **monetary tightening** – would be expected to slow the rate of growth of money and credit, and thus slow the economy. Reducing interest rates would represent a **monetary loosening.**

Monetary policy, like fiscal policy, has changed significantly in emphasis and scope in the post-war period.

- During the 1950s and 60s it was seen as an adjunct to fiscal policy in the task of **demand management.**
- In the 1970s and 80s it became the dominant instrument of *macroeconomic policy*, aimed at the goal of achieving and maintaining low inflation.
- In the 1990s this remained the role of economic policy, with the exception of the period from October 1990 to September 1992, when sterling was in the European **exchange rate mechanism** (ERM) and the pound's level drove monetary policy.

The operation of monetary policy changed significantly in May 1997 when, soon after the Labour party's election victory, the Chancellor of the Exchequer announced **operational independence** for the Bank of England. The government would set an official **inflation target,** currently 2.5 per cent, for the **underlying inflation** rate (measured by the retail prices index excluding mortgage interest payments), but decisions on the level of interest rates to achieve it would be taken independently by the Bank's **monetary policy committee.**

The decision to give the Bank operational independence, discussed in more detail below, was the culmination of a process in which *monetary policy has become the main weapon of short-term economic management, while fiscal policy concentrates on medium- and long-term issues.* Thus, while the level of interest rates can be changed from month to month, tax and public spending changes are much less frequent. The government now sets its public spending plans for three years ahead and tax changes are seen to be most important in the way they influence incentives and the supply side, as well as the distribution of income. Thus, when action has to be taken to boost or slow the economy, the onus is on monetary policy.

How does monetary policy work?

The easiest way of thinking of monetary policy is to remember that the interest rate represents the *price* of money, and that the higher the price the lower the demand. Raising interest rates reduces the **demand for money,** lowering them increases it. The demand for money, or **liquidity preference schedule** in Figure 10, demonstrates this effect. When interest rates are reduced from r_1 to r_2, the demand for money increases and the money supply increases from M_1 to M_2.

How does this work in practice? After all, in an economy there are both borrowers and savers. A fall in interest rates reduces, for example, the monthly mortgage payments of borrowers but it also reduces the income of savers. Why should not these two effects simply cancel one another out?

The reason why lower interest rates boost the economy is that borrowers have a higher **marginal propensity to consume** than savers. A young family with a mortgage is more likely to spend the proceeds of an interest rate reduction than an older person with savings is to increase spending in response to an interest rate rise. Lower interest rates also stimulate investment by companies. For an investment project to be worthwhile, companies have to be sure they can more than cover the cost of their borrowing. The lower the interest rate cost of borrowing, the greater the number of investment projects that will become viable.

In an open economy such as Britain, which trades a high proportion – just over 30 per cent – of GDP, the exchange rate is also an important **transmission mechanism** for monetary policy. A reduction in interest

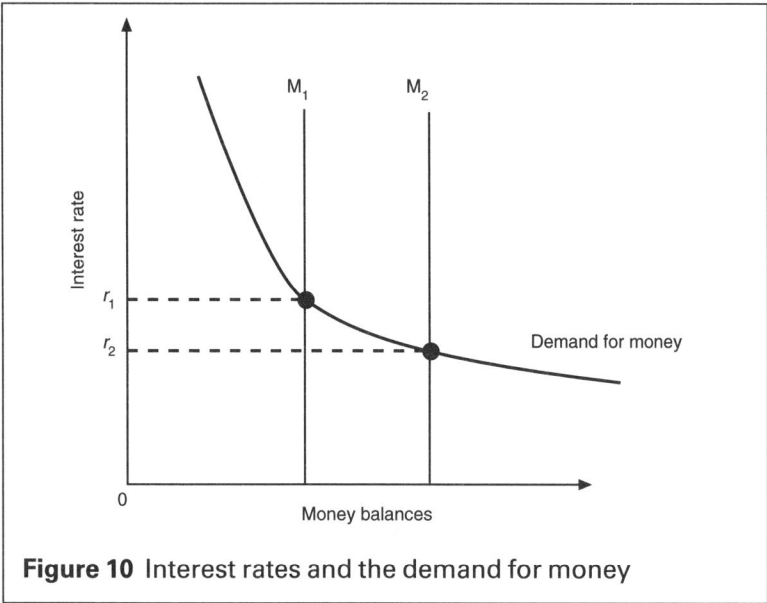

Figure 10 Interest rates and the demand for money

rates will tend to reduce the level of the pound, because it becomes less rewarding for international investors to keep their money in UK assets. A fall in the value of the pound can stimulate economic growth by making it easier for exporters to sell in overseas markets, and for British companies to compete against imports at home.

Monetarism and the role of the money supply

Monetarists believe the money supply is the key variable in the economy. The faster the growth in the money supply, the faster the growth of GDP in money terms. But, since the economy can grow only so far in real terms because of supply-side constraints, eventually too rapid a rate of growth in the money supply will lead to higher inflation.

Milton Friedman, perhaps the most influential modern-day monetarist, said:

> 'There is perhaps no other empirical relation in economics that has been observed to recur so uniformly, under so wide a variety of circumstances, as the relation between substantial changes in the stock of money and in prices; the one is invariably linked with the other and in the same direction.'

Friedman's modern **quantity theory of money** describes this relationship in terms of the following equation, or identity:

$$M \times V = P \times Y,$$

where M is the stock of money (changes in that stock being the money supply), V is the velocity of circulation (the number of times a unit of money is used in a given time period), P is the level of prices, and Y is real (inflation-adjusted) GDP.

The Conservative government of Margaret Thatcher embarked on a monetarist strategy for controlling inflation. It believed that by setting targets for the money supply, and keeping to them, it could control inflation. Unfortunately, this proved easier said than done.

At the same time as wanting to control the money supply, the Thatcher government abolished a number of controls on the economy which had been used by previous governments to regulate money and credit flows. These included **exchange controls**, abolished in October 1979, which opened the possibility for British banks to supply loans to their customers in Britain from overseas subsidiaries. The government also abolished (a) the so-called banking **'corset'**, properly called the supplementary special deposits scheme, which restricted the rate of growth of bank lending; and (b) **hire purchase controls**, which limited the amount individuals could borrow, usually for the purchase of cars and consumer durables.

The result of these actions was that the only weapon left for controlling the money supply was interest rates. These rates initially rose very sharply, to 17 per cent, but this proved to be of mixed success.

The government also fell victim to **Goodhart's Law**, invented by Professor Charles Goodhart, then a senior Bank of England official, now a member of the monetary policy committee. He said that any measure of the money supply targeted by the authorities automatically becomes distorted.

The Bank of England still produces figures for the growth in the money supply, mainly **M0** (M-zero), which consists largely of notes and coins, and **M4,** a far wider measure, which includes notes, coins, and all bank and building society deposits.

Monetarism was, however, abandoned in the 1980s and, following the 1990–92 experience of ERM membership, has now given way to the setting of inflation targets.

Bank of England independence and the inflation target

Prior to May 1997, when the Bank of England was granted operational independence, decisions on interest rates were taken by the Chancellor of the Exchequer, usually but not always in consultation with the Bank.

Monetarism faces crisis as Britain's economy plunges

ANGUS MCCRONE

Not so long ago monetarism was so fashionable as an economic theory that everyone from Margaret Thatcher and Ronald Reagan to a generation of young-buck economists in the City and academia claimed allegiance. They all believed that you had only to control the money supply and the rest of the economy would fall into line.

Monetarism was so dominant that money-supply figures were covered by the main evening television news. The statistics came in many guises – M0, M1, M2, sterling M3, M4. About the only one that did not seem to exist was M25. Opponents coined the phrase "sado-monetarism".

Since its heyday in the early eighties, the theory has continued to exert a strong influence on policymakers. The fact that the late-eighties' boom and bust in Britain took place after former Chancellor Nigel Lawson ignored warning signs from the money supply figures ensured that his successors would be more vigilant.

Now, however, monetarism is in crisis. Money is supposed to be a leading indicator of inflation and output growth. Yet the broad measure of money supply, M4, has continued to grow strongly this autumn (a trend that would normally point to rising inflationary pressure), while the British economy has gone into a steep dive.

Monetarism has not covered itself in glory elsewhere either. In Japan, the most expansionary monetary policy in history – with interest rates close to zero – has failed to spark any economic recovery. In Germany, control of interest rates by Bundesbank monetarists has coincided with four million unemployed. So is monetarism a busted flush, or could the followers of Milton Friedman have the last laugh?

The City's top monetarist, Tim Congdon of Lombard Street Research, admits: 'I think there is indeed something of a crisis for monetarism. Normally with high money growth, you would expect strong domestic demand growth and inflation.' Congdon believes, however, that the fact that strong British M4 growth – 9.1 per cent in the year to October – is sending us important messages, namely that the economic downturn in 1999 should be mild and that there will be strong support for the London stock market if it falls sharply.

Non-monetarists are not convinced. Roger Bootle, author of *The Death Of Inflation*, says: 'Contrary to monetarist propaganda, it has never been the case that there is a clear and unambiguous relationship between money, output and inflation. The chain of causation can work the other way round, with money figures lagging behind real economy indicators.'

After expanding slowly in 1992–94, M4 accelerated rapidly and grew at 10 per cent or so a year from 1995 to 1997. It has slowed in 1998, but still remains above the top of the monitoring range defined by former Tory chancellor Kenneth Clarke, and well above the 5 per cent level that might be compatible long term with inflation of 2.5 per cent.

Monetarist Patrick Minford, of Liverpool Macroeconomics, is sceptical about the money data. He says financial deregulation has 'played fast and loose with broad money' and that narrow money, or M0, has been distorted by the spread of hole-in-wall cash machines and by low interest rates, which make people prepared to hold more notes and coins.

London Evening Standard, 15 December 1998

For the period from the autumn of 1992 (sterling's expulsion from the ERM) to May 1997, the Bank's role was formalized. It was required to produce a quarterly **inflation report**, setting out its predictions for inflation, and there were regular monthly meetings between the Chancellor and his officials and the Bank's Governor and his staff. With Kenneth Clarke as Chancellor and Eddie George as Governor, these became known as 'the Ken and Eddie show'.

The minutes of these meetings were published, to show what advice the Bank had given, and how the Chancellor's decision had been arrived at. The Chancellor, while operating under a self-imposed inflation target of 1–4 per cent, was not under any obligation to accept the Bank's advice.

In the months leading up to the May 1997 election, Clarke consistently refused to raise interest rates – citing the strain on industry as a result of a rising pound – despite being urged to do so by both the Bank and his own Treasury officials. Critics said this demonstrated the shortcomings of a system in which interest rates were subject to political control, although subsequent evidence, and in particular a sharp slowdown in the economy, were seen by his supporters as vindicating Clarke.

After May 1997, with the Bank granted operational independence, monthly meetings to set interest rates continued, but this time only the Bank's monetary policy committee (MPC) took part – there was no political involvement.

The nine-member MPC consisted of five Bank officials – the Governor, two deputy governors, its chief economist, and the director responsible for financial and money markets. Four more economists were appointed by the Chancellor as 'outside' members of the MPC.

In 1999, the committee consisted of Eddie George (Governor), Mervyn King and David Clementi (deputy governors), John Vickers (chief economist), Ian Plenderleith (executive director responsible for markets), Sir Alan Budd (former Treasury chief economic adviser), Professor Willem Buiter of Cambridge, Professor Charles Goodhart of the London School of Economics, and DeAnne Julius (former British Airways chief economist).

As in the 1992–97 period, the MPC's task now is to achieve an inflation target, this time of 2.5 per cent for underlying inflation excluding mortgage interest payments. In setting the target, the Chancellor stressed that it was *symmetrical* – in other words that it was as bad to overshoot the target as it was to undershoot it. The Governor is required to write a letter of explanation to the Chancellor if inflation exceeds 3.5 per cent, or if it falls below 1.5 per cent. The minutes of the

MPC's deliberations are published two weeks after the meetings.

In order to arrive at its decisions, on which there is always a vote, the committee considers a wide range of evidence, including the following.

The economy's growth rate in relation to its long-run trend (2.25 per cent a year) and its position in the economic cycle

If the economy were growing significantly above trend and had done so for a number of years, so that spare capacity had been used up, the MPC would tend to raise interest rates.

Economists use the **output gap** to try to measure whether there is spare capacity in the economy. At the top of the economic cycle, the output gap is likely to be small, and continued strong growth will tend to be accompanied by higher inflation. The MPC determined that this was the position in 1997/98.

The labour market

Sharply falling unemployment is an indication that the economy is approaching capacity, and a rise in pay settlements would be interpreted by the MPC as a warning signal of inflation ahead.

Commodity prices

Commodity prices, such as those of oil and other raw materials, will tend to be influenced not by the strength of demand in Britain, but rather by world economic developments.

Movements in the exchange rate

A falling value of the pound will tend to raise import prices and add to inflation in Britain.

The recent inflation performance

Although interest rate decisions are forward-looking, they will be influenced by whether inflation is currently above or below the target.

Monetary growth

This is represented by the growth in the monetary aggregates, M0 and M4, and in bank lending, mortgage demand and consumer credit.

Asset prices

The faster asset prices are rising– such as house prices and the stock market – the more this is likely to be evidence of inflation in the system, or of a future rise in demand (because people can borrow and spend on the back of rising housing or stock market wealth).

To see how these factors influence the committee's decisions, the minutes are available on the Bank's website: www.bankofengland.co.uk

Is independence better?

Part of the reason why the Chancellor chose to give the Bank of England control of interest rates was to free himself for other aspects of economic policy, notably tax reform and improving the economy's long-run performance.

There is also, however, a strong belief, supported by research, which suggests that over the long-term independent central banks deliver low inflation, without sacrificing economic growth. A 1993 study by A. Alesina and L. Summers, *Central Bank Independence and Macroeconomic Performance: Some Comparative Evidence*, showed that countries which have had independent central banks for a long period, such as Germany and the USA, have performed better.

Other research has suggested that, in the early stages of bank independence, the trade-off between growth and inflation can be worse than before. An example is given by New Zealand, which made its central bank independent in 1989.

Figure 11 shows that both inflation and interest rates have been low in Britain since about 1993, but that this did not begin with Bank of England independence.

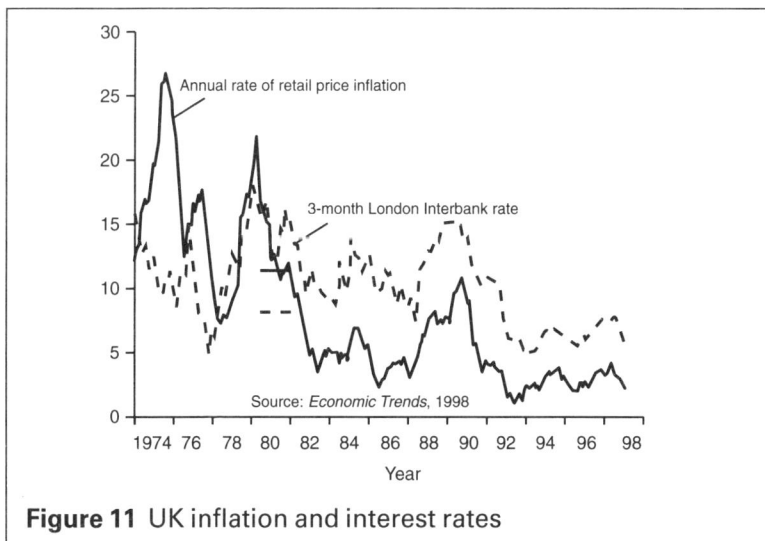

Figure 11 UK inflation and interest rates

How Bank of England independence compares with other countries

The Bank of England is operationally independent in that it operates monetary policy in order to achieve the inflation target (2.5 per cent) set for it by politicians. In other countries, central banks are left to judge for themselves what targets to achieve. The German Bundesbank, for example, operated a broad definition of price stability, and usually attempted to achieve it by setting targets for the money supply. The same is true for the Federal Reserve Board in the USA.

Another key difference concerns the decision-making committee of the Bank. In the USA, representatives from the regional federal reserve banks take part in the decisions. In the case of the European Central Bank, six council members are from the central directorate, but 11 are from the national central banks of the participating countries. Because there is no federal structure in Britain, interest rate decisions are taken centrally, a factor the Bank tries to compensate for by ensuring that reports from its regional agents affect its decisions.

Transparency is another important issue for central banks. The Bank of England is one of the most open and transparent central banks in the world, issuing the minutes of its decision-making meetings two weeks later and publishing a quarterly inflation report. The European Central Bank is less transparent, not publishing its minutes at all, for fear that the national central bank representatives who help make decisions on interest rates would come under undue pressure if it so.

What will happen to monetary policy if the UK joins the euro?

By the time the Bank of England obtained operational independence it had been in existence for more than 300 years. Many economists, however, believe the current period of independence will be short-lived, because the UK government will decide over the next few years – following a public referendum – to join the European single currency.

Joining the euro would be different from previous currency arrangements that the UK has entered. During the period 1990–92, when the government was required to keep sterling within a specified range against other European currencies in the European exchange rate mechanism, the Bank could be instructed to keep interest rates at whatever level was needed to achieve that aim. In the end, even raising UK rates to 15 per cent in September 1992 was not enough to prevent the pound from crashing out of the ERM.

Joining the euro would be quite different. Not only would the pound's level against other European currencies be permanently fixed – and sterling itself would disappear as a separate currency – but interest rates would no longer be set in Britain. The Governor of the Bank of England would simply become a voting member of the decision-making council of the European Central Bank (ECB).

At present there are 17 such members. If the UK and no other country joined the euro, the Governor would have one vote among 18 on the ECB council. Thus, the two traditional weapons of monetary policy, interest rates and the exchange rate, would be determined at a European level, rather than a UK level.

This is why the Maastricht treaty emphasized convergence of inflation, interest rates and budget deficits – together with a prolonged period of exchange rate stability – as prerequisites for joining the single currency. Interest rates would still be set for Britain by an independent central bank, but it would now be the European Central Bank.

KEY WORDS

Monetary conditions	Liquidity preference schedule
Interest rates	Marginal propensity to
Exchange rate	consume
Money and credit	Transmission mechanism
Monetary tightening	Quantity theory of money
Monetary loosening	Exchange controls
Demand management	'Corset'
Exchange rate mechanism	Hire purchase controls
(ERM)	Goodhart's Law
Operational independence	M0, M4
Inflation target	Inflation report
Underlying inflation	Output gap
Monetary policy committee	Transparency
Demand for money	

Reading list

Atkinson, B., Livesey, F. and Milward, R., Chapter 21 in *Applied Economics*, Macmillan, 1998.

Beardshaw, J. *et al.*, Chapters 37 and 38 in *Economics: A Student's Guide*, 4th edn, Addison-Wesley Longman, 1998.

Heathfield, D. and Russell, M., *Inflation and UK Monetary Policy*, 3rd edn, Heinemann Educational, 1999.

Smith, D., *The Rise and Fall of Monetarism*, Penguin, 1987.

Useful website
Bank of England: www.bankofengland.co.uk/

Essay topics

1. (a) How does the Bank of England attempt to influence interest rates? [12 marks]
   (b) Discuss the role of monetary policy in controlling inflation. [13 marks] [Associated Examining Board 1998]
2. (a) Why might a country wish to restrain inflationary pressures? [40 marks]
   (b) Examine the policies which a member country of the EU might use in an attempt to prevent an increase in the domestic rate of inflation. [60 marks] [University of London Examinations and Assessment Council 1997]

Data response question

This task is based on a question set by the University of Oxford Delegacy of Local Examinations in 1997. Read the piece below and study the table. In answering the questions that follow you should use not only the information given, but also your own knowledge of economics, economic analysis and economic institutions.

Low inflation

In the UK, despite rises in raw material and import prices, plus higher indirect taxation, retail prices in general have barely moved. Why? The obvious answer is, of course, the effect of the recession on consumer spending, together with the flood of 'special offers' and discounts that have become available.

Another way of looking at it is to suppose that business can opt for either a 'high-price, low-output' or 'low-price, high-output' strategy. In many sectors there is an understanding that the second strategy is the more profitable. Customers are now acutely price sensitive, as they were not when inflation was high and companies could become complacent and inefficient. It is generally held that low price inflation benefits the consumer and the economy in general.

But is this necessarily the case? One way of keeping prices low is to be ruthless in keeping costs down, and this may mean shedding labour as well as keeping wages low. Moreover, firms are more likely to expand by means of horizontal mergers, which may bring about economies of scale, than by taking the risk of introducing new products. Such policies may hold down household real incomes and increase monopoly power.

Yet a look at the success of economies such as Germany and Japan indicates that it is possible to combine low inflation with growth and high employment. The problem for the UK is how to do this too.

Table A International economic performance (percentages)

	Growth rate*	Growth per head†	Inflation‡	Unemployment ¶
Japan	4.3	3.6	1.5	2.5
Spain	3.2	2.9	8.7	22.7
USA	3.1	1.7	3.9	6.7
UK	**2.8**	**2.4**	**5.7**	**10.2**
Italy	2.4	2.2	9.1	11.5
Germany	2.3	2.4	2.7	8.2
France	2.3	1.7	5.4	11.6
Netherlands	2.1	1.6	1.7	7.5
OECD average	2.6	1.6	5.0	8.1

* Annual average growth rate of GNP, 1980–91

†Annual average growth rate of GNP per head, 1980–92

‡ Average annual growth of inflation, 1980–92

¶ Unemployment rate, 1993

Source: *Human Development Report 1995*.

1. (a) What is meant by the phrase 'customers are now acutely price sensitive'? [4 marks]
   (b) Give *two* explanations why consumer sensitivity to price appears to have increased in the UK. [4 marks]
2. Explain in what type of market businesses may have a choice of a 'high-price, low-output' or 'low-price, high-output' strategy. [16 marks]
3. (a) Explain why 'It is generally held that low price inflation benefits the consumer and the economy in general'. [16 marks]
   (b) To what extent do the data provide support for the view that a low-inflation environment is an important ingredient of successful economic performance? [22 marks]
4. Compare the effectiveness of lowering interest rates or increasing government expenditure as methods of achieving both low inflation and high employment. [18 marks]

Chapter Five

Modern full employment

'The government's strategy is to provide employment opportunity for all – the modern definition of full employment for the twenty-first century – through: a framework for macroeconomic stability and growth; programmes to help people from welfare to work; tax and benefit reform to make work pay; investment in education and skills; and a flexible and adaptable labour market.'
Financial Statement and Budget Report, HM Treasury, March 1998

Measuring unemployment

Unemployment statistics are a source of intense debate. Traditionally, unemployment in Britain was measured by the **claimant count** – the number of people out of work and claiming benefit. Critics said that this represented only a partial measure of unemployment because it excluded many people who were out of work but not entitled to benefit, for example some married women wishing to return to work or excluded from benefit because of their husband's earnings.

On some estimates the difference between the two measures was large. The trade unions and some economists suggested true unemployment in Britain in the late 1990s was more than four million, even when official figures showed under two million. To add to the confusion, in the 1980s there were regular changes in the method of calculating the figures, which tended to reduce the official total.

Despite this, the claimant count rose and fell sharply in the 1980s, only to repeat the pattern in the 1990s. Figure 12 shows this.

The Labour government elected in May 1997 responded to criticism of the claimant count by publishing a new monthly unemployment figure based on the **Labour Force Survey (LFS)** and in line with internationally-agreed **International Labour Office (ILO)** definitions.

This new measure, based on whether people were available for work, did not show unemployment above four million, but it did show a total nearly half a million higher than the claimant count. In early 1999, the claimant count stood at 1.3 million (4.6 per cent of the workforce) and the LFS measure was more than 1.7 million (6.2 per cent).

For 1998, LFS unemployment was 6.8 per cent in Britain, while unemployment rates on the comparable (ILO) measure were 4.8 per

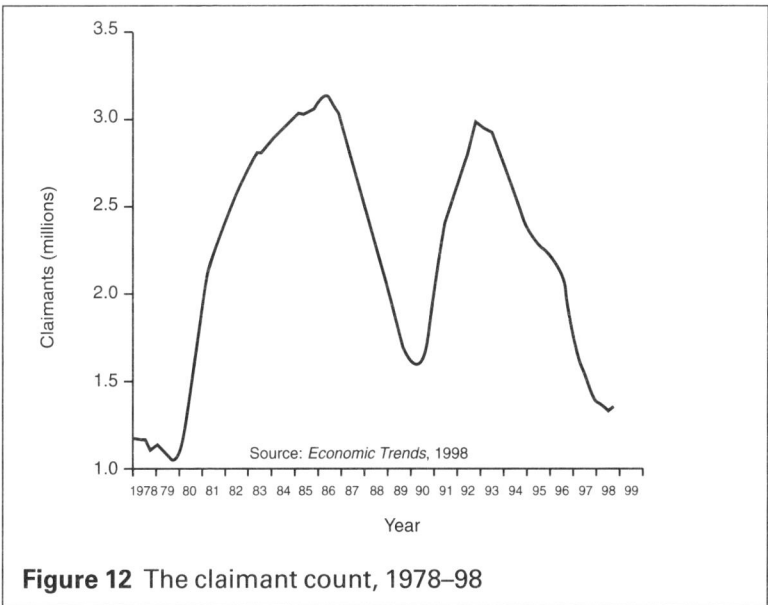

Figure 12 The claimant count, 1978–98

cent in the USA, 11.9 per cent in France, 11.5 per cent in Germany and 3.5 per cent in Japan. The EU average was 10.5 per cent.

Comparative figures for unemployment, and other economic data, are published by the Organization for Economic Co-operation and Development (OECD). Its website is at www.oecd.org.

Traditional full employment

Economists traditionally defined 'full' employment as being equivalent to an actual unemployment rate of 2–3 per cent, because in practice there will always be some unemployment, of various types:

● **frictional unemployment,** when people are temporarily out of work because they are moving between jobs

● **seasonal unemployment,** because some work depends on the weather and the time of year

● **structural unemployment,** caused by changes in the industrial structure of the economy, and the fact that it takes time to adapt the skills developed for one industry to another

● **regional unemployment,** because it is unlikely that labour market conditions will be the same in all parts of the country; for example, the south-east of England could have full employment while there is still high unemployment in the north, as happened in the late 1980s.

Voluntary and involuntary unemployment

One of the central differences between the approaches of Keynesian economists and those favouring a monetarist or supply-side view is over the *causes* of unemployment.

- Keynesians typically argued that unemployment was usually **involuntary,** and explained by insufficient aggregate demand in the economy. The solution was thus for governments to boost demand.
- Monetarists or supply-siders believe most unemployment is **voluntary,** and caused by the fact that workers are not prepared to accept lower wages – they price themselves out of jobs.

Whatever happened to full employment?

After the very high unemployment of the inter-war years – the Great Depression – Britain and most other industrialized countries had two decades of virtually full employment in the 1950s and 60s. But from the early 1970s, full employment became an increasingly distant goal, and rising unemployment was accompanied by rising inflation. The economy experienced long periods of **stagflation** – slow growth or recession leading to high unemployment but accompanied by high inflation.

World economic conditions

World economic conditions were much more difficult. The two oil price shocks provoked by OPEC (Organization of Petroleum Exporting Countries) in 1973/74 and 1979/80 led to world recession. Britain experienced slower growth: just 2.25 per cent a year in the 1970s and 1.6 per cent during 1980–93.

Inflation

Inflation was no longer subdued. The oil price shocks, together with rising world commodity prices, produced an externally generated inflation stimulus.

Unemployment and inflation

The **unemployment/inflation trade-off** (see below) worsened – higher levels of unemployment were associated with higher inflation than in the past. This was due to the above factors, but also to (a) strengthened trade union power and militancy in the 1970s, and (b) structural problems, notably the decline in manufacturing employment. Manufacturing employment has declined from nine million in 1970 to under four million in the late 1990s. Only in the 1990s was there sufficient growth in service-sector employment to compensate.

Policy emphasis

The policy emphasis shifted. Initially when unemployment rose, policymakers attempted to expand their economies to reduce it. In Britain this led to the Barber boom in 1972/73 under the Conservative government of Edward Heath, and the failed attempt by Denis Healey, Labour Chancellor in 1974–79, to boost the economy in the wake of the first OPEC oil crisis. In 1976, Britain was forced to call on the assistance of the International Monetary Fund (IMF) and control of inflation became the new orthodoxy.

Demographic changes

Demographic changes were unhelpful. In particular the 'baby-boomers' of the 1960s entered the labour market in the late 1970s and the 1980s, expanding the available workforce and creating a serious problem of youth unemployment.

The international unemployment problem

Since the early 1970s, high unemployment has not been a problem only in Britain. In fact, compared with many other industrial countries the UK fared relatively well in the 1990s. As Figure 13 shows, unemployment throughout the industrialized world – the OECD is a grouping of nearly 30 industrial countries – rose sharply in the 1970s and 80s, eventually reaching more than 30 million.

In 1994 the OECD published its *Jobs Study*, analysing the reasons for high unemployment. It concluded that employment growth in North America, at 1.8 per cent a year since 1960, had been far stronger than in Europe, where it had been only 0.3 per cent.

The OECD said high unemployment, particularly in Europe, could not be blamed on new technology – the idea that people have been replaced by machines was not supported by the evidence. It also rejected the charge that unemployment in the industrialized countries was caused by imports from low-wage economies, or by increased global competition – so-called *globalization*. It recommended measures for countries to adopt to reduce unemployment. They were:

- setting macroeconomic policy in a way that keeps control of inflation but which takes advantage of any slack in the economy to achieve more rapid economic growth
- promoting the more widespread use of technology
- increasing working-time flexibility, for example by encouraging firms to open up more opportunities for part-time work

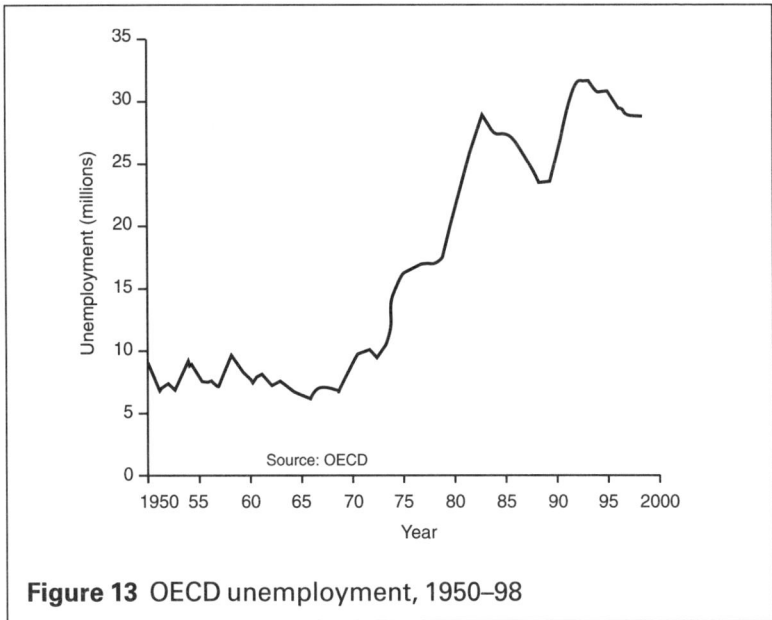

Figure 13 OECD unemployment, 1950–98

- nurturing an 'entrepreneurial climate' by removing the obstacles to the setting-up and expansion of businesses – small businesses have been responsible for a substantial amount of job creation
- making wages more flexible, for example by allowing younger workers to be taken on at lower wages
- making it less onerous for companies to reduce staff – the more difficult it is to fire people, it was argued, the less willing firms will be to hire them in the first place
- using 'active' labour market policies, such as Britain's New Deal, to make the transition from welfare into work easier
- improving education and training systems in order to raise skill levels in the labour force – the evidence is that the unskilled have suffered most from rising unemployment
- reforming unemployment benefits, as well as other aspects of welfare – if welfare payments are too generous, there may be little incentive for workers to take on a job.

Since publishing the *Jobs Study*, the OECD has regularly published a scoreboard on the progress of countries towards achieving these aims. In general, the USA – which started in an advantageous position – has done well, as have the UK, Ireland and the Netherlands. Other

Labour changes approach to unemployment

CHRISTINE BUCKLEY

David Blunkett, the Education and Employment Secretary, has demoted one of the great shibboleths of the Labour Left, full employment and job security for all.

The government will tomorrow set out a £112 million plan to help the long-term jobless with the creation of 12 employment zones. But in an interview with *The Times* today, Mr Blunkett says full employment is unrealistic.

He says: 'I don't think there will ever be full employment in the old sense of the word, where you had a job for life, you had great security, it was a full-time job. I think the challenge is to meet people's desire to work but in a much more adaptable way than previously.'

Mr Blunkett will launch the unemployment zones to provide extra help for people who have been out of work for a year or 18 months. The zones will channel resources from existing initiatives – such as European funds, regeneration cash, training and enterprise councils – along with new cash from the Department for Education and Employment and the Department of Social Security, into one pool.

The employment zones will give the unemployed personal job accounts that will enable spending via a personal adviser to help to get people back into work. Mr Blunkett says this is the first time that all the resources have been pooled to help the jobless. The zones will be implemented after testing the scheme in five pilot areas and will run for two years from next year. They will target about 48 000 people. Half of the zones will target those who have been unemployed for a year, while the other half will tackle those who have not worked for 18 months.

Mr Blunkett says the zones will tackle the most urgent unemployment blackspots.

The 12 zones are: Birmingham, Brent, Brighton and Hove, Doncaster, Haringey, Liverpool and Sefton, Middlesbrough and Redcar and Cleveland, Newham, Nottingham City, Plymouth, Southwark, and Tower Hamlets.

The Times, 1 February 1999

countries in Europe have made little progress, including Germany and Italy, which suffered high unemployment in the 1990s.

The unemployment/inflation trade-off – the Phillips curve

The **Phillips curve** owes its name to Professor A. W. Phillips, an engineer-turned economist who published an important paper in 1958 called 'The relationship between unemployment and the rate of change

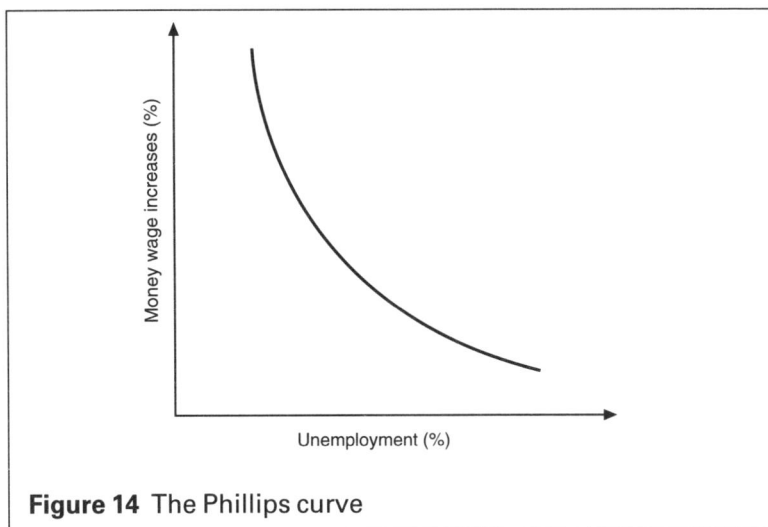

Figure 14 The Phillips curve

of **money wage rates** in the United Kingdom, 1861–1957'. Figure 14 shows a typical Phillips curve.

The price of labour (wages), he said, depends on the demand for labour. When unemployment was high, demand for labour would be weak and its price would stay low, implying small pay rises. But when unemployment was low, demand for labour would be strong, and firms would seek to outbid each other for scarce labour, pushing up pay.

There would thus be a trade-off between wages and unemployment. In addition, because wages were a key element in setting prices – many economists favoured a so-called **cost-push** explanation of inflation – there was an inverse relationship between inflation and unemployment.

The natural rate and the NAIRU

How can the Phillips curve explain the simultaneously rising unemployment and inflation of the 1970s and 80s? After all, the Phillips curve suggests a trade-off between the two.

Milton Friedman, the monetarist economist responsible for the modern quantity theory of money, provided an alternative approach, using the Phillips curve framework. He said there was a **natural rate of unemployment** for the economy, determined by factors such as:

● the efficiency of the labour market, including the mobility of labour and the extent of trade union **restrictive practices**

- the generosity or otherwise of unemployment benefits (the more generous, the higher the natural rate)
- education and training levels among the workforce.

If unemployment is below this natural rate, then demand for labour outstrips supply, and **real wages** (wages adjusted for inflation) are bid higher. If unemployment is above the natural rate, real wages fall.

This sounds like the traditional Phillips curve, and Friedman accepted that in the short term there was a trade-off between unemployment and the growth of wages. His key innovation was to focus on real wages rather than money wages.

Consider a situation in which a government has pushed unemployment below its natural rate by boosting the economy. Initially, real wages are pushed higher. But then adverse effects creep in. Inflation also rises, so eroding the initial rise in real wages. Workers notice what has happened and are determined not to get caught out again. Their expectations of inflation have changed. The change in expectations as a result of experience is rational behaviour: economists describe this as **rational expectations**. Next time they will want an even bigger increase in wages to compensate for an expected increase in inflation. This is illustrated in Figure 15.

Assume that we begin on the lower of the short-run Phillips curves. The government attempts to push unemployment below its natural rate

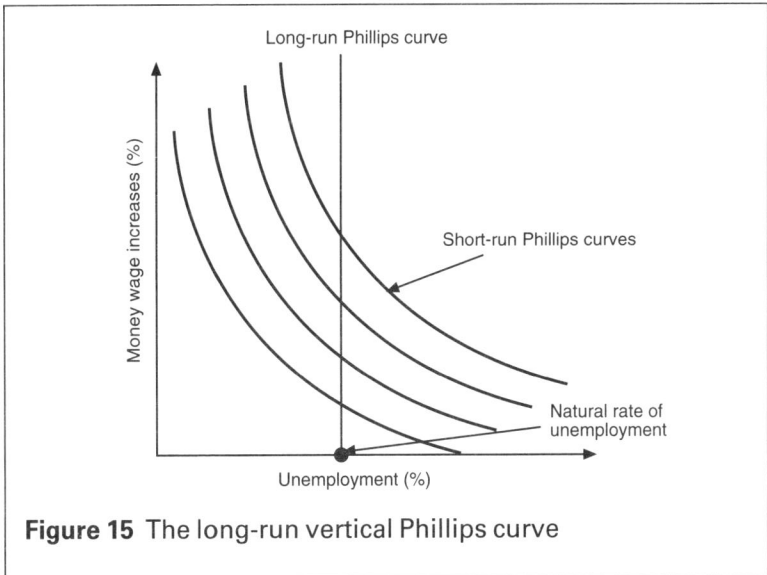

Figure 15 The long-run vertical Phillips curve

and initially succeeds, at the expense of higher money wage increases. The impact of these higher money wage increases are, however, higher inflation, and the government is forced to act to slow the economy. The next time the government seeks to reduce unemployment below its natural rate, workers will be wise to the higher inflation that is likely to result and will demand higher money wage rises to compensate. The economy moves to a higher short-run Phillips curve, and so on, each time gravitating towards the natural rate of unemployment.

In the long run the Phillips curve is vertical – unemployment can be reduced below its natural rate only by supply-side measures, for example those which increase the flexibility of the labour market.

The non-accelerating inflation rate of unemployment (NAIRU)

Modern economists prefer to use the NAIRU in preference to the natural rate, because the latter somewhat callously implies there is something 'natural' about even very high levels of unemployment. In addition, while the natural rate came from monetarist thinking, the NAIRU is employed by all schools of economic thinking. Monetarists would place emphasis on supply-side factors, while Keynesians would say that demand factors can influence the level of the NAIRU.

To give an example of the latter, many economists believe that if governments and central banks run economic policy too tightly for a prolonged period, and push unemployment higher, this can increase the NAIRU. This is because, the longer that people are out of work, the more difficult they find it to get back in, because their skills become rusty and their confidence is eroded. *Prolonged unemployment can breed unemployment, and a rise in the NAIRU.* Some economists call this effect 'hysteresis'.

The NAIRU can be used to gauge policy. If policymakers allow unemployment to rise above the NAIRU, in the belief that this is necessary to control inflation, this is policy **overkill**. The opposite of trying to drive unemployment below the NAIRU is **underkill**.

The NAIRU is not easy to estimate. In the late 1990s, Britain's NAIRU was estimated to be 7 per cent on the ILO measure (see above), but unemployment fell below that without an acceleration in inflation.

Reducing the NAIRU – the Conservative approach

It is a desirable aim of policy to reduce the NAIRU, so that the economy can operate with a better unemployment/inflation trade-off. In the 1980s and for some of the 1990s, Conservative administrations under Margaret Thatcher and John Major placed much of their emphasis in reducing the NAIRU on trade union reform. Beginning in 1980, a series of parliamentary acts acted on the power of the unions by:

- restricting the 'closed shop' – the requirement that all employees of a particular firm must belong to a union
- making it more difficult for unions to start industrial action
- reducing the financial power of unions, and making them legally responsible for the financial consequences of their actions
- enhancing union democracy, both for the election of officials, and in the case of ballots for industrial action
- reducing the political role of the unions, by outlawing secondary action (when unions strike in support of workers in other organizations) and political action.

The union reforms coincided with a period of sharply declining union membership, from a peak of 13.3 million in 1979, to under eight million by the late 1990s. There was also a sharp decline in days lost owing to strikes and other forms of industrial action. Although the trade-off between unemployment and inflation did not improve in the 1980s, many economists believe these reforms were responsible for some of the improved trade-off in the 1990s.

Reducing the NAIRU – the Labour approach

While the Labour government elected in May 1997 left in place most of the union reforms it inherited, it introduced some policies that were seen to be reversing the trend – notably the **European social chapter** which increased workers' rights.

Labour also embarked on a new strategy, that of reducing the NAIRU by acting directly upon the supply of labour. The **New Deal**, financed by a £5 billion windfall tax on the privatized utility companies (electricity, water, gas, etc.), sought to bring excluded workers back into the workforce. Those aged between 18 and 24 years and unemployed for more than six months were offered one of four options – a job, training, a return to education, or a place on the government's environmental taskforce – with no 'fifth option' of remaining on benefit. Similar offers were made to unemployed people in other age groups out of work for more than two years, and to lone parents.

In essence, the New Deal offers the unemployed a subsidized return to work, in the hope that this will overcome the problem of 'unemployment breeding unemployment'.

The Labour government has also tried to increase the supply of labour, and reduce the NAIRU, by trying to overcome the **unemployment trap** caused by the operation of the benefits system. If available jobs are low-paid, and if people, particularly those with families, find that in taking up those jobs they are no better off than when they were on benefit, there is no incentive for them to take up work. The unemployment trap keeps them out of work.

The **working families' tax credit** (WFTC), like the system of family credit it replaces, attempts to overcome this. People are given a pay 'top-up', courtesy of taxpayers, to give them an incentive to take up a low-paid job. The theory underlying it is that, once in work, they will tend to advance to better-paid jobs, and the tax credit they need will be reduced. The government calls this approach 'a hand-up rather than a handout'. It remains to be seen how big the effect will be. The Institute for Fiscal Studies suggested the WFTC would increase the supply of labour by between only 10 000 and 45 000 people.

Modern full employment

It can be seen that the approach to full employment has changed. In the 1950s and 60s, governments believed that, by varying the demand in the economy, they could achieve full employment – an unemployment rate of 2–3 per cent. Now it is recognized that demand is not the only factor, and that supply-side factors are also important.

Apart from the fact that it would be a hostage to fortune for any modern politician to commit to full employment, there is recognition that the supply-side measures needed to bring it about – to reduce the NAIRU – are likely to take a long time. Hence the Chancellor's description of modern full employment as 'employment opportunity for all'.

KEY WORDS

Claimant count	Money wage rates
Labour Force Survey	Cost-push
International Labour Office	Natural rate of unemployment
Frictional unemployment	Restrictive practices
Seasonal unemployment	Real wages
Structural unemployment	Rational expectations
Regional unemployment	NAIRU
Involuntary unemployment	Overkill
Voluntary unemployment	Underkill
Stagflation	European social chapter
Unemployment/inflation trade-off	New Deal
	Unemployment trap
Phillips curve	Working families tax credit

Reading list

Anderton, A., Unit 92 in *Economics*, 2nd edn, Causeway Press, 1995.

Clark, A. and Layard, R., *UK Unemployment*, 3rd edn, Heinemann Educational, 1997.

Davies, B., Hale, G. and Tiller, H., Chapter 4.26 in *Investigating Economics*, Macmillan, 1996.

Paterson, I. and Simpson, L., *The UK Labour Market*, 2nd edn, Heinemann Educational, 1998.

Useful website

OECD: www.oecd.org/

Essay topics

1. (a) Explain how an increase in government spending can result in a greater change in the equilibrium level of national income. [10 marks]

   (b) A government is faced with an unacceptably high level of unemployment, but does not wish to increase its overall expenditure. Discuss alternative policies for reducing the unemployment. [10 marks] [OCR, The National Economy Paper, 1998]

2. Many people have been out of work for more than a year. Evaluate the economic policies that might be used to reduce unemployment in such circumstances. [40 marks] [Oxford, 1998]

Data response question

This task is based on a question set by the Oxford and Cambridge Joint Examinations Board in 1996. Read the following piece, which is adapted from an article by Diane Coyle published in the *Independent* in March 1996. Then answer the questions that follow.

The debate about unemployment

Unemployment in Britain has fallen for 29 consecutive months, but the fact that 2.2 million people are still out of work is one of the causes of insecurity for many of the 28 million people in the workforce. Yesterday the Bundesbank announced that German unemployment had set a new post-war record of 3.97 million. But there is little consensus about solutions to the problem because economists have wildly different views about how the labour market works. Patrick Minford (Liverpool University) believes that Conservative policies have reduced the *natural rate of unemployment*; the labour market works better and can now deliver lower equilibrium unemployment. It would be still lower if demand since 1990 had been greater.

However, Andrew Britton (Churches Inquiry into Unemployment) is more sceptical, believing that the jobless total cannot fall much below two million without triggering accelerating inflation and current account problems. This suggests that most unemployment is structural and not cyclical. This leaves him to explain why deregulation and deunionization seem to have helped unemployment to fall in Britain and the USA since the recession when it has not fallen in the more heavily regulated labour markets in Europe.

Richard Layard (Labour party adviser) focuses on the long-term unemployed (those out of work for over a year) who constitute 40 per cent of the total. He argues that taking action to get these people back to work would not have an adverse effect on inflation because they are *for all practical purposes out of the labour market*. He proposes that the government should guarantee jobs for the long-term unemployed, by offering subsidies to private sector firms. The main counter-argument is that they would simply replace people who already have jobs; Layard disputes this by claiming that the labour market *would adjust accordingly*.

Most economists deny that the labour market adjusts in a classical sense, and see unemployment as the result of a variety of *market failures*. A further issue (raised by Britton) is whether we even know what 'full employment' means any more; the post-war definition would certainly *be very different now*.

1. Define 'natural rate of unemployment'. [2 marks]
2. Why, in 1996, was unemployment falling in the UK when it was rising in most other EU countries? [4 marks]
3. What is the basis of the disagreement between Minford and Britton? [4 marks]
4. Why does Layard consider the long-term unemployed 'for all practical purposes out of the labour market'? [4 marks]
5. What does Layard mean when he claims that the labour market 'would adjust accordingly'? [3 marks]
6. What 'market failures' might cause unemployment to persist? [4 marks]
7. Why might the definition of full employment 'be very different now'? [4 marks]

Chapter Six

Stability and economic growth

'The government's new macroeconomic framework has helped the UK economy to become more resilient and provides a defence against the return to "boom and bust". The new framework provides not only the means to avoid unnecessarily large fluctuations in activity caused by excessively short-term policy decisions, but also allows responses that limit the adverse effects of external shocks.'
Pre-budget Report, HM Treasury, November 1998

The business cycle

When economists talk of the business cycle, they are referring to the economy's tendency to display a regular pattern over time. This pattern can be simply stated. Beginning in the upswing or **recovery** phase, individuals and companies gradually grow more confident about their own and the economy's prospects, forgetting about the previous **recession**. They are prepared to borrow more, for spending and investment, and in doing so they push the economy's growth rate up – there is an increase in aggregate demand. Eventually, unchecked, the recovery turns into a **boom**.

The boom leads to higher inflation and, usually, balance of payments problems (strong growth in spending sucks in imports). The government responds by tightening fiscal policy, and the Bank of England responds by raising interest rates, in order to slow the economy, and the economy enters a **downturn** or recession, when it has slowed to the point at which policy can be relaxed again. This and the fact that, after a period of weak spending, companies and individuals need to spend to replace worn-out machinery and equipment, or household goods and cars, gives the next cyclical upturn.

This type of business cycle, with four or five years separating each cyclical **peak** or **trough**, has been identified during much of the post-war period. It is necessary, however, to refine it to cover modern experience.

There have been three serious recessions since 1973 (1974–75, 1980–81 and 1990–92) that were harsher than anything before in the post-war period. In the first two of those cases, external factors – notably a sharp rise in world oil prices – played a major role. Prior to those recessions, economists believed **Keynesian demand management,** operating fiscal and monetary policy in a counter-cyclical way, had succeeded in dampening down the economy's cyclical variations.

The harsher post-1973 experience has led to a change in the definition of recession. Previously used to describe a period of declining growth (for which we now use *downturn* or '*growth recession*') a recession is now defined as at least two quarters of falling GDP. **Depression** (or slump) is not the same as recession. A depression occurs when an economy reaches a cyclical trough *and remains there*. The last UK depression was in the 1920s and 30s. Japan in the 1990s has experienced conditions close to those of a depression.

Figure 16 shows recent British cyclical experience, including the 'boom' of the late 1980s, the 'bust' of 1990–92, and the steadier growth since then.

Theories of the business cycle

Economists, long fascinated by the business cycle, have put forward different explanations of why it occurs. Indeed, they have identified different kinds of cycle, including the 'long wave' thesis of Nikolai Kondratieff, a Russian economist, who believed that each upswing

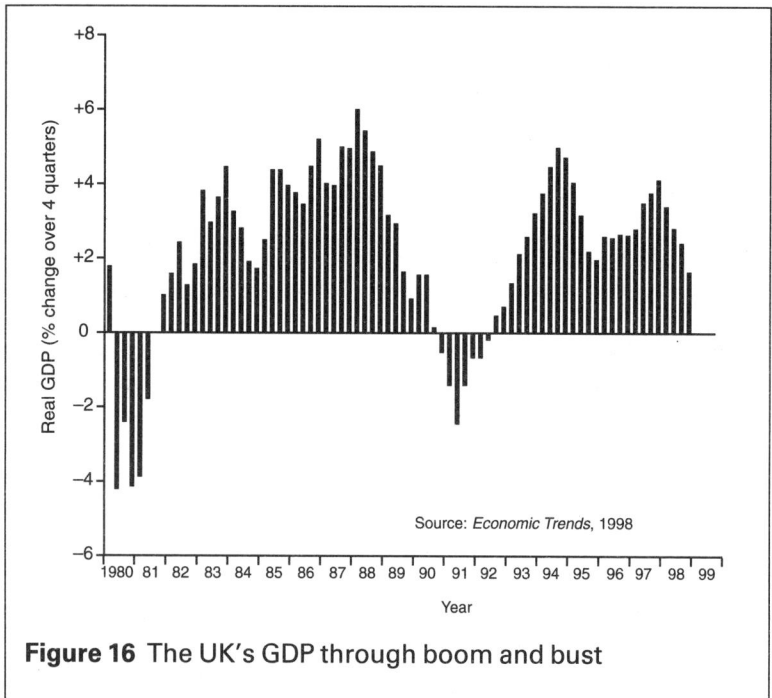

Source: *Economic Trends*, 1998

Figure 16 The UK's GDP through boom and bust

lasted for around 25 years, and was followed by a downswing of similar length.

In the 1970s, when the world economy embarked on weaker growth after two decades of strong expansion, many thought it marked the beginning of a Kondratieff down-wave. However, while unemployment has been higher since the early 1970s than before, and growth more erratic, it would be going too far to characterize it as a down-wave.

● Keynesian cycles

Staying with the more conventional business cycle, Keynesian economists emphasize the role of the **multiplier** and the **accelerator**. Producers respond to a small increase in demand by making a proportionately larger increase in investment in the machinery that makes it. *This is the acceleration principle*. The effect of this investment increase is to further boost demand throughout the economy through the *multiplier principle* (the initial stimulus comes from higher income and employment among the people making the machines).

Thus, an initial small demand increase is amplified in its impact, producing a build-up in economic growth, and eventually a boom. But when demand turns down, perhaps because of a policy tightening, accelerator effects are reversed – entrepreneurs cut investment in new plant and equipment disproportionately and multiplier effects operate in the opposite direction.

● Monetarist cycles

Monetarists believe that the business cycle is caused by variations in the rate of growth of money. An increase in the money supply initially leads people to spend more, because they feel better off. But when inflation rises, they realize that their money holdings (so-called 'real money balances') have been eroded in value. Thus, after the rise in spending, there is a period during which people rein back to rebuild their real money balances. Thus we have a spending cycle, and hence a business cycle.

Monetarists argue that the best way of ensuring that cyclical variations in economic activity are small is to maintain steady growth of the money supply.

● New classical cycles

New classical (neoclassical), or supply-side, economists believe that business cycles are caused by unanticipated **shocks**. These can be of the kind identified by Keynesians, an increase in demand leading to additional investment, or by monetarists, a money supply increase producing an initial increase in demand; or they can be the kind of 'external' shock such as a rise in world oil prices, which hit Britain in the 1970s.

New classical economists differ from the others because they believe there will always be such shocks, and that the business cycle cannot be avoided.

Traditional counter-cyclical policies

The demand management policies of the post-war period were driven by a Keynesian view of business cycles. If demand in the economy, both consumption and investment, is cyclical, then the policy response is clear: government itself has to compensate for such demand changes.

Thus, during a boom the government reins back on its own spending and other spending over which it has control – for example, investment by nationalized industries. It, or the central bank, increases interest rates. In a recession, the government 'primes the pump' by boosting its own investment and current spending, and interest rates are reduced.

Politicians used the analogy of driving a car. A 'little touch on the brake' would slow the economy, while a 'dab on the accelerator' would speed it up. Modern politicians are more humble about their ability to steer the economy – their favoured analogy is of piloting an oil tanker, with each change in direction taking some time to have an effect.

A scaled-down version of traditional counter-cyclical policies is that of allowing the economy's **automatic stabilizers** to operate. Tax revenues fall during a downturn and public expenditure tends to rise (notably because of higher payments of unemployment benefits). Rather than trying to increase tax rates or reduce other elements of public spending to offset these developments, the government allows these automatic stabilizers free rein. This means that even if the government is determined to rein back on public spending as a long-term aim, it does not do so in a recession for fear of making things worse.

Britain's cyclical experience

According to the Treasury, Britain has had more pronounced economic cycles than other industrialized countries – the economy has been more unstable. In its November 1998 Pre-budget Report the Treasury said:

> 'In each of the last two economic cycles, Britain's economic performance was poor compared with other G7 countries [the Group of Seven consists of the world's seven most important

industrial economies – the USA, Japan, Germany, France, Britain, Italy and Canada]. *During this period, the UK had one of the highest average inflation rates and below-average growth. Fluctuations in output and inflation were higher than elsewhere, with growth ranging from minus 2 per cent to plus 5 per cent and inflation from 2 to 21 per cent. Interest rates and fiscal deficits were almost twice as volatile as those in France, Germany and the USA. All this damaged businesses' and consumers' ability to plan ahead effectively. It also contributed to Britain's poor productivity growth.'*

This more volatile record can be explained by a number of factors, and most notably errors in both monetary and fiscal policy. In November 1997, the Treasury published a paper 'Fiscal policy: lessons from the last economic cycle' – it is available on the Treasury's website (www.hm-treasury.gov.uk). This concluded that the Conservative government at the time underestimated the extent to which an improvement in the public finances – a shift from fiscal deficit to surplus – was due to cyclical factors. Thus, the government continued to cut taxes even as the economy boomed, believing that the strength of the public finances justified this approach. When the economy slowed markedly, the government boosted public spending to try to compensate, but the main effect of this, combined with a cyclical deterioration in the public finances, was to produce a record budget deficit (then measured by the public sector borrowing requirement) of £46 billion or 7 per cent of GDP, in the early 1990s.

The Treasury's chart, showing where the economy was in relation to its long-term trend in both the boom and the subsequent bust, is reproduced as Figure 17.

The Treasury concluded that there were two main lessons from that experience:

- *Lesson 1:* Take a prudent approach. Adjust for the economic cycle and build in a margin for uncertainty.
- *Lesson 2:* Be open and transparent. Set stable fiscal rules and explain clearly fiscal policy decisions.

Fiscal policy errors are not the only explanation for Britain's greater volatility compared with other countries. Serious mistakes were also made in monetary policy. In the late 1980s boom, interest rates were cut to 7.5 per cent at the height of the boom in 1988, before being raised sharply to 15 per cent only 18 months later. According to the Treasury:

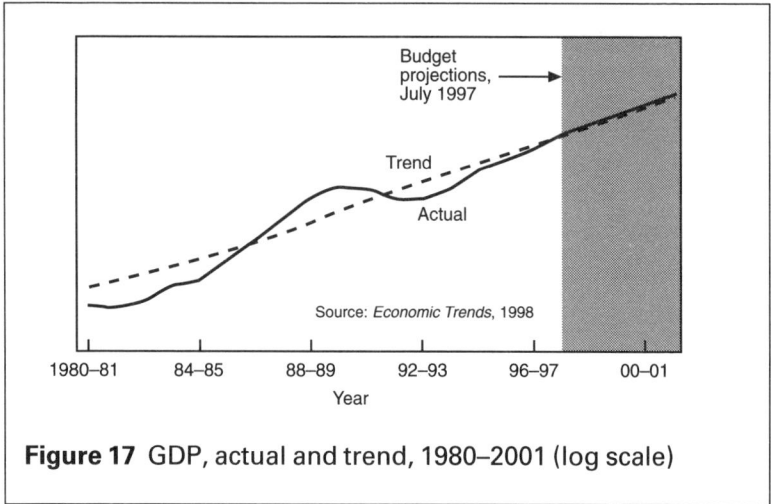

Figure 17 GDP, actual and trend, 1980–2001 (log scale)

'*The UK's relatively large cyclical behaviour reflects, in part, the consequences of policy mistakes as fiscal and monetary policy decisions were taken without a clear framework and with changing objectives. Required corrective action was typically not forthcoming until it was too late, resulting in greater than necessary problems and excessive corrective action.*' (Pre-budget Report, November 1998)

Most of the increase in Britain's cyclical volatility, in addition, has come during the era of floating exchange rates. As an open economy which trades around 30 per cent of its GDP, and with a currency which is heavily traded, volatility in sterling has tended to transmit itself to the rest of the economy.

Does cyclical volatility hamper growth?

The Treasury, as noted above, believes that Britain's record of having more pronounced cycles than other countries has adversely affected economic growth. There are a number of reasons why this might be:

- Companies are cautious about committing too much investment, for fear of being caught out by a sharp downturn. Insufficient investment is a prime reason for Britain's GDP per head and productivity performance compared with other countries.
- Companies may also be cautious about hiring and training staff, because they fear having to lay them off in the next downturn.

Never a boom, but real risk of bust

David Smith

Harold Macmillan once likened running the economy on the basis of official statistics to planning a train journey using last year's Bradshaw.

Just as bad workmen blame their tools, so bad policymakers, perhaps with more justification, blame poor statistics. If the data say one thing, but the reality is different, no wonder there are errors.

I say this because Britain's economic statistics are about to undergo far-reaching changes. Under what the Office for National Statistics (ONS) describes as the biggest changes in the national accounts since 1952, the story of the economy is to be rewritten.

Has British business been under-investing in relation to competitors? Yes, according to those, including Gordon Brown, the Chancellor, and his advisers, who say short-termism has held the economy back. But the new figures, will for the first time include computer software as part of investment. This makes sense – the old treatment, in which a computer was investment but not the software that might make it more efficient, was illogical – and it could change perceptions about the level of business investment.

An even more important change in perceptions could come with the new data. There has been a story going round that the economy was in the middle of an unsustainable boom when Kenneth Clarke handed it over, and only their swift action averted disaster.

But this has been a strange sort of boom. Like that strange television series of a few years ago it has had twin peaks. The first, in 1994, saw growth hit 4 per cent on the back of the post-exchange-rate-mechanism boom in exports. The second, in 1996–97, was a more conventional consumer-led affair, but it was modest.

Inflation did not take off and the balance of payments did not plunge into a gaping deficit.

Now, according to the ONS, it may have been even less of a boom than it looked. The national accounts will include the re-basing of recent GDP data to 1995. Re-basing tends to reduce measured growth because those sectors growing fastest tend to have the strongest productivity growth and lowest price rises. Their weight in the new calculations of GDP is correspondingly reduced.

The ONS says this will reduce the economy's cumulative growth between 1994 and 1997 by between 1 and 2 per cent.

If there never was much of a boom, does there have to be much of a downturn? Is there, in other words, an economic equivalent of the old adage that the bigger they are, the harder they fall?

Sadly not. The deepest recession since 1945, in 1980–81, came not after a boom but after the economy's steady recovery from the crisis that required International Monetary Fund help in 1976. A less-than-exuberant boom is no protection from a savage bust.

Sunday Times, 30 August 1998

- The belief that inflation is always about to return means that workers negotiating pay are always looking to anticipate the next rise in prices, perhaps more than in other countries.
- Economic volatility encourages investors to seek safe havens for their money. In Britain, a relatively high proportion of investment has gone into housing – 'bricks and mortar' – at the expense of productive investment.

Professors Charles Bean and Nicholas Crafts, in a book *Economic Growth in Europe Since 1945* (Cambridge University Press), found that in Britain government policy could be criticized for its 'short-termism' in seeking immediate results when inflation or unemployment rose, rather than pursuing a long-term strategy for economic growth. As such, it may have been a contributory factor in Britain's relative growth and productivity record. More important factors were, however, education and training and, at least until the Conservative reforms introduced under Margaret Thatcher, the poor industrial relations climate.

Government policies for stability

Tony Blair and Gordon Brown have pledged that there will be 'no return to boom and bust', and have introduced policies aimed at ensuring that the short-termism mentioned above will not shape economic policy.

In particular, Bank of England independence, with the Bank required to focus on achieving the official inflation target of 2.5 per cent, not only takes the politics out of interest rate decisions but is also intended to ensure that monetary policy is set in a medium-term context. It remains to be seen how successfully this will work. Although there is evidence that countries that have had independent central banks over a long period have less volatile economies (as well as generally lower inflation), it is not clear whether this is as a result of central bank independence or other factors. In the winter of 1998/99, when the economy was slowing sharply and the inflation threat was seen to be receding sharply, the Bank's monetary policy committee reduced interest rates quickly, just as a 'political' Chancellor of the Exchequer wishing to avert recession would have done.

The Labour government's other main innovation has been on fiscal policy. In the summer of 1998, the Chancellor announced a three-year public expenditure settlement for government departments, with spending to rise by 2.75 per cent a year in real terms. The idea, he said, was to allow departments to plan properly for the future, but also,

Budgetus prudens: Gordon Brown making a virtue of fiscal prudence

significantly, to keep a rein on any temptation he might have to relax spending further in response to short-term economic difficulties or pre-election political considerations.

The Chancellor also published a **Code for Fiscal Stability**, a legally-binding framework based on five principles – transparency, stability, responsibility, fairness and efficiency – requiring the Treasury to report regularly to Parliament on developments affecting the public finances, and committing the government to two long-term fiscal rules.

- **The Golden Rule** means that over the economic cycle, the government will borrow only to finance investment, not current public spending (which must be financed out of taxation).

- **The Sustainable Investment Rule** requires the government to maintain net public sector debt, which in 1999 was 40 per cent of GDP, at a 'stable and prudent level' over the cycle.

The test for the new monetary and fiscal policy frameworks will be firstly, whether they can be kept to, and secondly, whether they make a difference in terms of the UK's cyclical volatility, or whether they are outweighed by other factors.

Deindustrialization and the economic cycle

One feature of recent UK economic cycles is that the manufacturing sector has suffered disproportionately. Figure 18 shows this at work.

Soon after Margaret Thatcher took office in 1979, the 1980–81 recession hit manufacturing hard. It was caused by a combination of high interest rates and an overvalued exchange rate. Output dropped by a fifth, and a similar proportion of industrial capacity was scrapped. In the 1990–92 recession, caused by similar factors, manufacturing also fared worse than the rest of the economy even though that recession was dubbed the 'white collar recession'. In the late 1990s, as the economy as a whole skirted recession, manufacturing again suffered a prolonged decline in output, although this was less pronounced than in the two previous downturns.

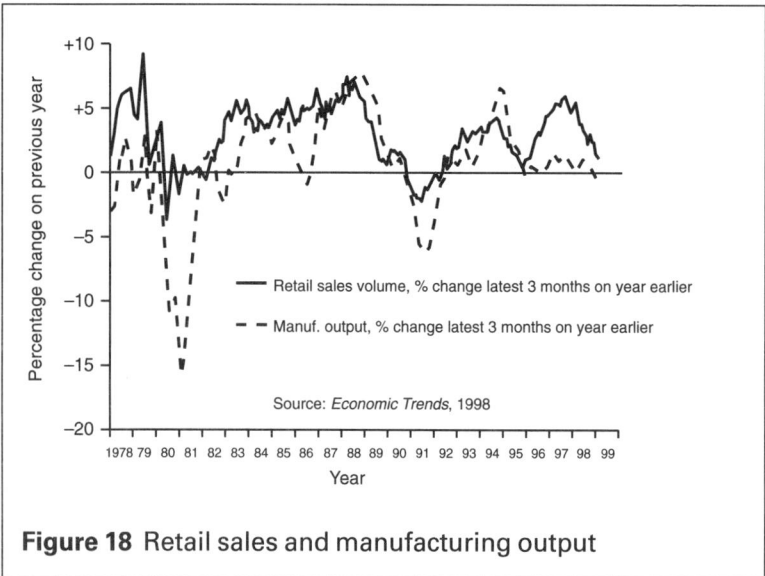

Figure 18 Retail sales and manufacturing output

Why does manufacturing suffer most? Most UK exports, about three-quarters, are of manufactured products. When a recession is caused by both high interest rates and a high exchange rate (and in a floating currency regime it is hard to have one without the other), industry is hit on both counts – the so-called 'double whammy'. High interest rates increase the cost of borrowing for manufacturers while the rise in sterling's external value makes it more difficult for firms to export. Domestic service-sector firms, on the other hand, suffer only from the high interest rates.

Why, then, do manufacturers not benefit when both interest rates and the pound falls? Sometimes they do.

In 1994, for example, manufacturing output rose strongly because interest rates fell; and the pound, following its 1992 departure from the European exchange rate mechanism, dropped to a highly competitive level at which it was easy for firms to export.

Cyclical variations in manufacturing output are, however, on top of another long-term trend, that of the declining importance of manufacturing (the 'secondary' sector, in favour of services (the 'tertiary' sector). Currently, manufacturing accounts for only just over 20 per cent of the UK economy, although many service-sector activities are also dependent on the manufacturing sector. In 1970, around nine million people were employed in manufacturing. This dropped to seven million by 1979, to five million after the 1980–81 recession, and to just over four million by the early 1990s.

At the time of writing, under four million people are employed in manufacturing. *Manufacturing has suffered from a higher level of cyclical volatility than the rest of the economy, while the process of deindustrialization means that the sector is in long-term relative decline.*

KEY WORDS

Recovery	Multiplier
Recession	Accelerator
Boom	Shocks
Downturn	Automatic stabilizers
Peak	Short-termism
Trough	Code for Fiscal Stability
Keynesian demand	The Golden Rule
management	The Sustainable Investment
Depression	Rule

Reading list

Buxton, T., Chapman, P. and Temple, P., Chapter 4 in *Britain's Economic Performance*, 2nd edn, Routledge, 1998.

Grant, S., *Economic Growth and Business Cycles*, Heinemann Educational, 1999.

Sloman, J., Chapter 13 in *Economics*, 3rd edn, Prentice Hall, 1997.

Smith, D., *From Boom to Bust*, Penguin, 1993.

Useful website

HM Treasury: www.hm-treasury.gov.uk/

Essay topics

1. (a) How might supply-side policies help to increase a country's rate of economic growth? [50 marks]
   (b) Evaluate the possible benefits and costs of a faster rate of economic growth in a country of your choice. [50 marks] [University of London Examinations and Assessment Council 1998]
2. (a) Explain how supply-side policies might be used to (i) reduce the level of unemployment, and (ii) increase the rate of economic growth. [70 marks]
   (b) To what extent have supply-side policies been effective in achieving these aims in the UK? [30 marks] [University of London Examinations and Assessment Council 1996]

Data response question

This task is based on a question set by the University of Cambridge Local Examinations Syndicate in 1996. Read the article below (by D. Wong), which appeared in *Straits Times* on 13 November 1993. Then answer the questions that follow.

Economy posts 9.2 per cent growth in third quarter

The Singapore economy grew by 9.2 per cent in the third quarter of this year [1993]. As growth remained broad-based, and the electronics industry and stock market are expected to continue their good performance, the government has raised its growth forecast for the whole year to about 9 per cent.

This is an improvement on its projection of 7.5–8 per cent annual growth made in August, which was itself a revision from an earlier forecast of 6–7 per cent.

The Ministry of Trade and Industry, however, expects economic growth to ease next year, and has made a tentative forecast of 6–8 per cent growth for 1994. A spokesman noted that the electronics industry was cautious and the construction sector was slowing down because of fewer contracts this year.

The manufacturing sector continued its strong and rapid growth, in particular the electronics and petroleum industries. Overall, the sector grew by 10.9 per cent. 'Overall growth was fuelled by both external and domestic demand, and productivity growth is now at a sustainable 5.2 per cent,' said the spokesman.

Industrialists and businessmen are moderately optimistic about the business prospects, according to the ministry's survey of business

Vital signs

	1st quarter	2nd quarter	3rd quarter
Economic growth	7.3%	10.4%	9.2%
No. of jobs created	16,300	12,500	19,100
Inflation	2.4%	2.3%	2.4%
Productivity	4.9%	7.5%	*5.2%

How the sectors performed

Financial services
$ 17.6%
Stock market boost moderated by slower bank lending

Construction
$ 8.4%
Construction contracts totalled $2.3 billion

Manufacturing
$ 10.9%
Biggest growth: electronics, petroleum industries

Commerce
$ 8.2%
Growth leader: robust entrepot trade

Transport and communication
$ 9.1%
Cargo and passenger traffic slowed

Business services
$ 3.9%
Generally upbeat except for fall in real estates sector

* Singapore's products are still competitive in international markets because productivity has kept pace with wage increases.

expectations for the fourth quarter. 'Businessmen are still concerned about the stagnated growth of the developed countries and growth will probably have to come again from the ASEAN countries and southern China,' said the ministry spokesman.

1. (a) Describe Singapore's growth record in the first three quarters of 1993. [1 mark]
   (b) How did the government's latest overall growth forecast of 1993 (see the article) compare with earlier estimates? [2 marks]
   (c) Why was this latest forecast likely to be the more accurate? [2 marks]
2. What can be deduced from the article about Singapore's economic relationship with the rest of the world in 1993? [3 marks]
3. (a) What was the relationship between changes in productivity growth and economic growth in Singapore? [1 mark] (b) According to the information, Singapore's productivity kept pace with wage increases. Explain the economic significance of this. [2 marks]
   (c) Consider the problems of any one method of raising productivity. [3 marks]
4. Evaluate the likely effects of a fast rate of economic growth in an economy [6 marks]

Chapter Seven

Productivity and competition

'Productivity – the quantity of output each of us on average produces – is a fundamental yardstick of economic performance. No economy can grow sustainably unless its productivity improves. And poor productivity condemns a nation to be held back. This is precisely the position in the United Kingdom. We are not as productive as our major trading partners, and the extent of our under-performance is very substantial.'
Pre-budget Report, HM Treasury, November 1998

What is productivity?

Productivity is usually measured as output per worker. When questions were raised in the late 1990s over the future of Longbridge, the Rover plant in Birmingham, it was pointed out that productivity at the factory – 33 cars per worker per year – was significantly lower than at other plants. The Nissan plant near Sunderland, perhaps the most efficient in Europe, produced 100 cars per worker per year.

Since aggregate output across all industries and services is equal to gross domestic product, productivity is a key determinant of **GDP per capita**, or **living standards**. The raw figures on output per worker may not, however, be that useful. The Longbridge workers may look unproductive, but they were probably operating with outdated machinery. In addition, while the Nissan cars were mainly assembled using components bought in from outside, the Rover factory made many of its engineering parts on-site. Thus, making a car was a more involved process there and the lower output per worker could have been expected. Nissan workers were still more productive than those at Rover, but probably by not as much as the initial comparison suggested.

There are other complications. A part-time worker cannot be expected to produce as much in a week or a year as his or her full-time counterpart. Thus, sometimes output per worker-*hour* is a better measure of productivity.

Measuring output is another potential minefield. Rolls-Royce workers produce fewer cars per year than their counterparts at mass production factories, but this does not mean they are less productive. Each car they produce is worth a lot more. It is necessary to calculate the **value added** in the production process to assess productivity more accurately.

Labour productivity is not, in addition, the only determinant of GDP per capita. A small, oil-rich state in the Middle East may have very high living standards but this reflects the good fortune of owning valuable mineral deposits, not high productivity.

As already mentioned, the amount of investment is also important. My productivity is raised because I am writing this on a modern computer rather than a manual typewriter. It is also possible to measure **capital productivity**, the amount of output produced for a given amount of investment.

Britain has tended to have lower labour productivity compared with other industrial countries, but higher capital productivity. If there were greater investment in the economy, labour productivity would be likely to rise, capital productivity to fall. Economists sometimes put these measures of productivity together to make what is called **total factor productivity**. The evidence is that on this measure the differences between countries is relatively small.

Why does Britain lag behind on productivity?

According to the Treasury, as Figure 19 shows, Britain suffers a serious productivity gap compared with other industrial countries. In particular, output per worker is about 40 per cent higher in the USA than in Britain, while France and Germany enjoy 20 per cent better productivity than Britain.

Some of the reasons for higher productivity in other economies appear to be intrinsic to the economies concerned. The sheer size of the US economy means, for example, that companies can have longer production runs and thus enjoy the benefits of **economies of scale**. A

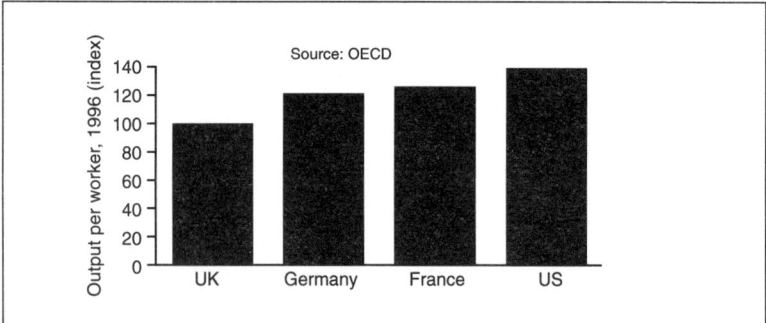

Figure 19 The productivity gap (UK = 100)

study in 1998 by McKinsey & Co., the international management consultants, found that one of the factors inhibiting productivity in Britain was that there were more planning constraints on businesses wishing to expand than in the US or France. In France, for example, it has been easier for new hypermarkets to open, while in the USA there is greater availability of land in general.

Most of the reasons for productivity differences are relatively straightforward. They include the following.

● Levels of investment per worker

Figure 20 shows that Britain's level of capital per worker (the amount of investment in machinery and equipment) is well below that of other industrial countries. According to the Treasury: 'The root of much of the productivity problem lies in a long history of under-investment.'

Not only do low levels of investment inhibit output per worker directly; they also limit the adoption of the latest, and most productive, techniques and technologies. Why has Britain had a relatively poor investment record?

Among the reasons identified by economists include:

● the City's 'short-termism', which has discouraged long-term investment by companies
● a banking sector which is also less supportive of investment by smaller firms than in other countries
● a relatively low level of savings as a proportion of GDP.

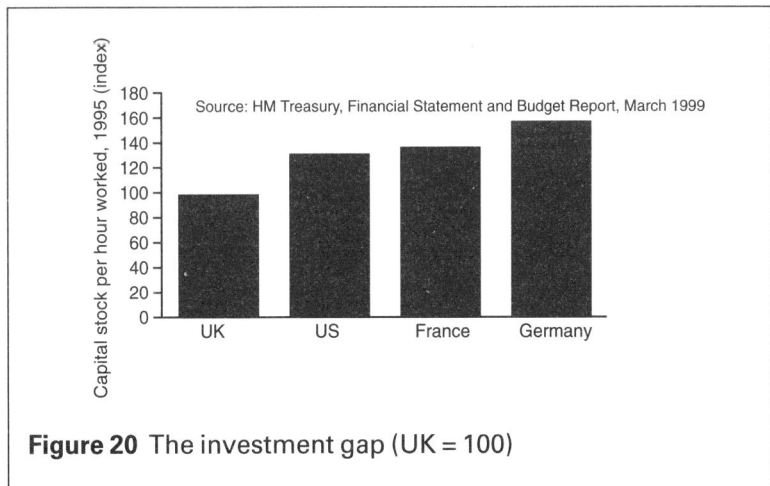

Figure 20 The investment gap (UK = 100)

Savings provide the funds for investment. Successive Chancellors have attempted to increase the level of savings by tax incentives such as Personal Equity Plans (PEPs), Tax Exempt Special Savings Accounts (Tessas), and now Individual Savings Accounts (ISAs).

Innovation

British companies, while investing less than their international counterparts, are also relatively poor at **innovation** – putting new ideas and methods into practice. This, again, has been a long-term problem.

While British scientists have been good at inventing things, which are often first put to commercial use overseas, British companies have been relatively poor at taking them up. Spending on research and development (R&D) is about 1.2 per cent of GDP in Britain, compared with 1.4 per cent in France, 1.5 per cent in Germany, 1.8 per cent in the USA and 1.9 per cent in Japan.

• Skills and education

Skills and education levels compare poorly with other countries. Britain has more early school-leavers – in 1995 only 54 per cent of 18-year-olds had stayed on in education in Britain, compared with 84 per cent in France and Germany. More than a fifth, 22 per cent, of adults in Britain have very poor literacy skills, compared with 14 per cent in Germany. Vocational skill levels are also poor, particularly in comparison with countries such as Germany, where there is a stronger tradition of training and apprenticeships.

• Macroeconomic instability

Britain's more volatile economic cycle, the greater tendency towards 'boom and bust' than in other countries, outlined in the previous chapter, has hampered productivity by discouraging companies from investing for the long term in new equipment, new methods and the training of workers.

• Lack of competition

Productivity and **competitiveness** are closely linked. A country with high productivity levels will generally be competitive in relation to others – it will be able to sell its products in direct competition with them. Much of British industry, on this view, was inefficient and uncompetitive in the past because it operated within a sheltered home market. Once trade was opened up to imports, these inefficiencies were exposed.

Thus, the British motorcycle industry was wiped out in the 1970s and 80s by competition from cheaper and more reliable Japanese imports. The same thing appeared to be happening to Britain's car industry until foreign manufacturers decided to set up in Britain and produce for themselves.

The Treasury believes that greater competition in Britain is needed to enhance productivity. 'The government believes that businesses deliver world-class innovative performance only when they are exposed to tough, open and fair competition,' it says.

Policies to boost productivity

Productivity underlines the comment made at the very beginning of this book, that policies which affect the economy extend over a wide range of government activity. They include policies to encourage more savings and investment, perhaps through tax incentives, and additional public spending on education and training – Tony Blair's 'education, education, education'. In 1998, the government announced a £19 billion boost to education and training spending over three years, setting new National Learning Targets and implementing a range of policies intended to promote lifelong learning.

As with most policies aimed at achieving productivity improvements, the likelihood is that the benefits of improving education and training standards will show through only over the long term.

Other measures include:

- the encouragement of employee share ownership, because people are believed to be more productive when they have a stake in the business
- new incentives for businesses, particularly small and medium-sized firms, to spend more on R&D
- the stability-orientated framework for macroeconomic policy, aimed at ending 'boom and bust', discussed in the previous chapter.

There is also a powerful role, if lack of competition is a factor holding back productivity, for competition policy, as will be discussed below.

Is there a trade-off between productivity and employment?

We know that labour productivity is generally measured as output per person. It follows that there are two ways of increasing productivity. One is to raise the level of output for a given number of workers. The other is to produce the same output, but with fewer people.

In the 1980s, a productivity 'miracle' was claimed in Britain, because the growth of manufacturing productivity was more rapid than in other countries. The components of this so-called miracle were

UK Productivity: economic agenda

BILL JAMIESON

When Gordon Brown launched forth on Britain's faltering productivity performance, backed up with selected slides from a McKinsey report, he must have thought he was on safe ground. But with every week that passes a little more falls away from the 'worst in G7' productivity thesis.

In truth, Britain's productivity gains have outpaced the global average since 1979. According to figures from the Organization for Economic Co-operation and Development for 1979–97, total factor productivity growth (value added per unit of labour and capital stock) in Britain averaged 1.2 per cent. This compares with 1.1 per cent for the OECD as a whole, 0.8 per cent for the Group of Seven industrial countries, and 0.6 per cent in Germany. On the OECD figures, Britain enjoyed the second highest productivity growth in G7 over this period.

Brown has taken more pessimistic figures, using them to convey the implication that Britain's economic performance in recent (Tory) years was relatively poor and that it is productivity failure, rather than higher taxes or higher interest rates, that lie behind the current downturn.

According to Michael Saunders, UK economist at Salomon Smith Barney, neither assertion holds true. Britain's 'productivity gap', he argues, dates back to 1950–80 and may reflect the rise in subsidies, labour market regulation and trades union membership in those years. The period saw relatively low rates of return on business capital and (probably as a result) sluggish business investment.

The productivity gap has been narrowing, not widening, in recent years. Since 1980, he points out, the UK's trend to lower public spending on subsidies, greater market deregulation and falling union membership has been associated with relatively high gains in rates of return on capital and the business investment/gross domestic product ratio – and fairly high productivity gains. The European Commission estimates that since 1979 the growth of UK GDP per head has roughly matched the EU average – and outpaced America, France and Germany.

Deregulation (as far as it goes with this government) and higher spending on education should help enhance productivity in due course. But other measures may undermine any improvement. The adoption of the EU working time directive will increase business costs by some £2 billion a year, adding 0.5 per cent to wage bills. The minimum wage will also add about 0.5 per cent to wage costs. More EU 'social model' measures are likely in the wake of Brown's embrace of the 'new European Way'.

Finally, the costly failure of the government's 'new deal' for the young unemployed hardly enhances its credentials on productivity. According to an analysis by Damian Green MP, each job created by the new deal costs the taxpayer a minimum of £11,333, while the cost of each job which can definitely be ascribed to it is £37,700. Almost one in four of those who have gone through the new deal, and who have not found a job, simply return to benefits. How very different Labour's performance looks once you penetrate through the spin.

Sunday Telegraph, 29 November 1998

interesting. In 1989, manufacturing output was barely higher than it was in 1979. Manufacturing employment had, however, fallen sharply – dropping from seven million to five million as a result of the 1980–81 recession, and falling further during the remainder of the 1980s.

The productivity improvements in the 1980s thus reflected lower direct employment in manufacturing. Some of this, in turn, occurred because firms engaged in outsourcing – where before they had employed catering, cleaning and maintenance staff, now they used contractors to perform such functions. Another reason for the improvement was the closure of inefficient firms. On the so-called 'batting average' argument, the closure of the least efficient factories will automatically result in a rise in average productivity levels.

Interestingly, as Figure 21 shows, productivity growth in manufacturing slowed in the mid-1990s, because firms were caught by surprise by a downturn in demand, and did not want to lay off staff.

It can be seen that there is a short-run trade-off between productivity and employment. In the long-run the most productive businesses and economies will be the most successful, and this will enable them to increase employment. *There is a limit to how much productivity improvements can be obtained by downsizing.*

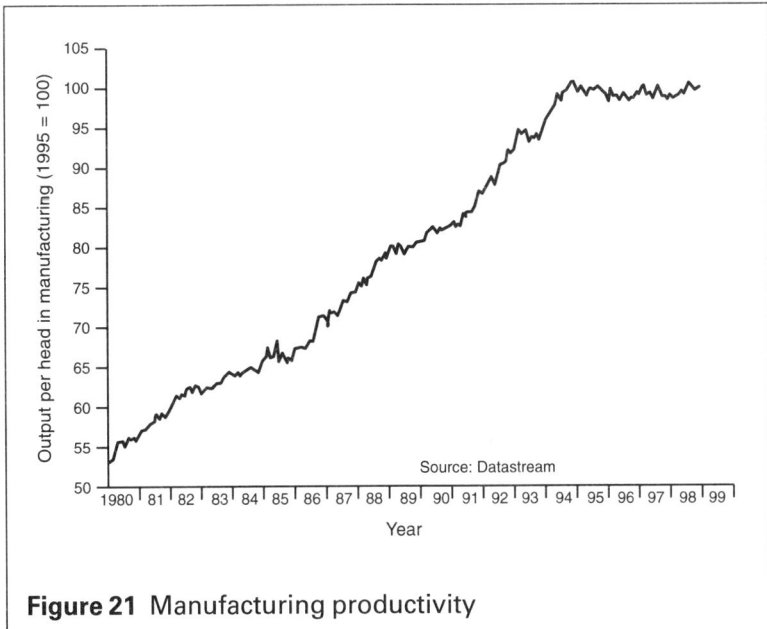

Figure 21 Manufacturing productivity

Productivity, competitiveness and the trade balance

Many economists would cite the gradual deterioration in Britain's trade balance as an indication of underlying problems in both productivity and competitiveness.

If productivity levels in the economy are relatively low, and wages quite high, then the competitiveness of British goods will suffer, in both home and export markets. Imports will undercut domestically produced goods, while exporters will lose market share overseas.

In the early 1980s, for the first time on a sustained peacetime basis since before the industrial revolution, imports of manufactured goods into the UK exceeded exports. This balance of trade in manufactures, once a source of strength for the UK economy, has continued in deficit since then. During the 1990s, Britain's overall deficit on trade in goods has averaged about £13 billion a year.

Is this proof of a problem of low productivity and a lack of competitiveness? Not necessarily.

When the UK first recorded a deficit on manufactured goods in modern times, in 1982, the country enjoyed a large surplus on trade in oil, thanks to North Sea production. One argument at the time was that the deficit on non-oil trade was a natural consequence of the surplus on oil trade, not least because one consequence of the UK's possession of huge oil reserves during that time of very high world oil prices was that sterling was pushed higher – it became a 'petrocurrency'.

Thus, what the UK gained as a result of the healthy surplus on oil, it may have lost on trade in non-oil goods, because the pound was pushed to too high a level to enable domestic firms to compete effectively.

Subsequently, while oil has become less important to the UK balance of payments, the deficit on trade in goods has generally been offset by a surplus on trade in services and other so-called 'invisible' items of trade. The UK, it appears, is a practical example of the law of **comparative advantage**. Greater resources have been shifted into services, where the UK appears to have a comparative advantage, and away from manufacturing, where it does not.

Thus, while the trade deficit in goods may be an indicator of competitive problems for certain sectors of the economy, it does not necessarily show that the economy as a whole is uncompetitive.

Competition

Economic theory shows that in conditions of **perfect competition**:

- there are large numbers of buyers and sellers
- no individual buyer or seller can affect the market price

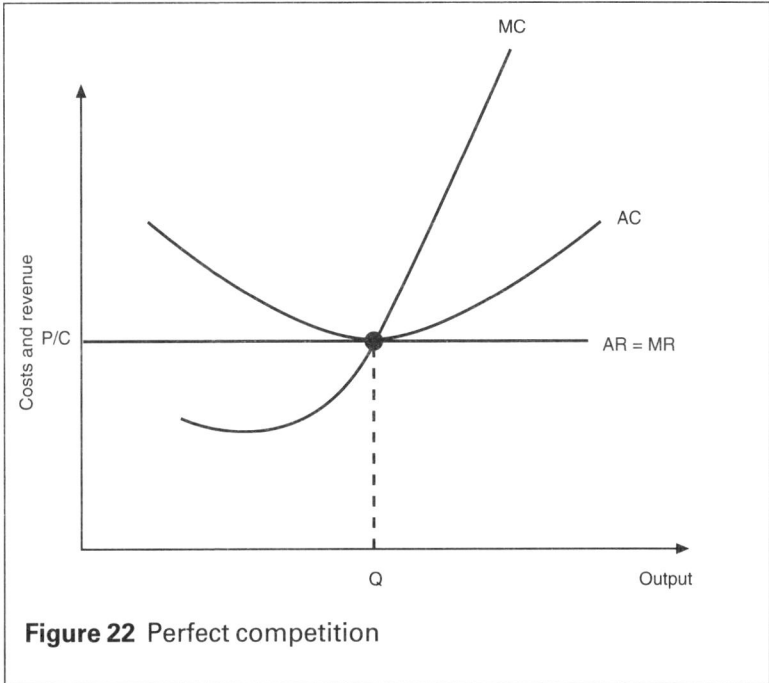

Figure 22 Perfect competition

- there is perfect information
- there are no long-run barriers to entry.

Figure 22 shows the standard long-run position for a firm operating in a perfectly competitive market. AC equals average cost, MC equals marginal cost, and the long-run average revenue (AR) and marginal revenue (MR) schedule is horizontal. Firms are price-takers. There are no supernormal profits. Now contrast that with the situation at the other end of the competitive spectrum – **monopoly**.

In contrast to the perfectly competitive firm, the monopolist is not a price-taker and faces a normal, downward-sloping demand schedule (AR in Figure 23). But, as the figure shows, the monopolist earns supernormal profits (the shaded rectangular area); and because there *are* barriers to entry, this situation persists in the long term. Under conditions of monopoly the price charged is higher, and the quantity produced lower, than in perfect competition.

Both perfect competition and pure monopoly are stylized examples. But even taking the contrast between the two, is it necessarily the case

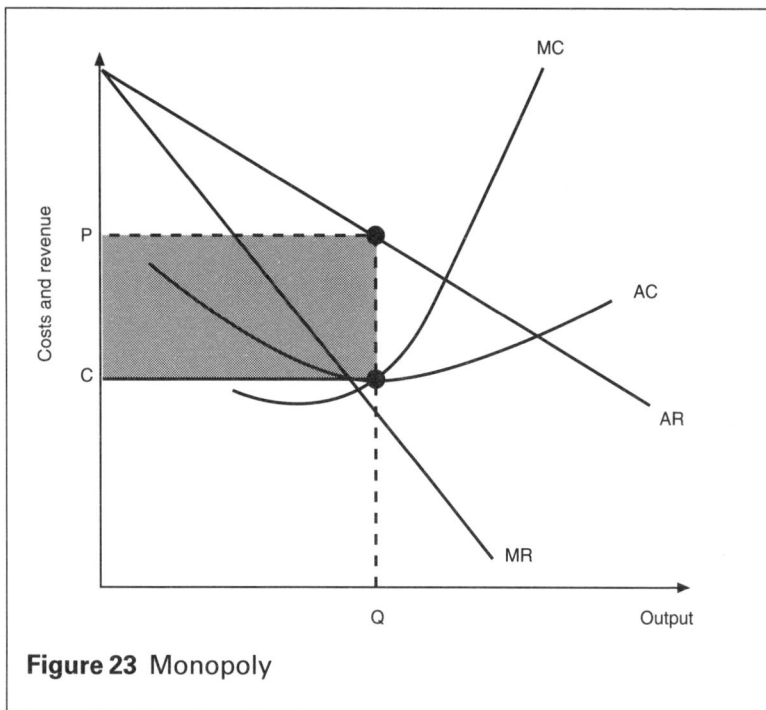

Figure 23 Monopoly

that monopolies are inefficient? After all, it may be that as a result of economies of scale the market will support only one producer.

Economists would argue, however, that this fact will be more than outweighed by other factors, notably:

- the lack of incentive for monopolists to invest and innovate
- the likelihood that, sheltered from competition, they will be inefficient.

Britain's former nationalized industries – British Rail, the National Coal Board, British Gas and the regional water and electricity boards – were inefficient for two reasons:

- they were protected monopolies
- they were not driven by the profit motive.

Privatization injected the latter, but only later was greater competition introduced.

Much of the criticism of privatization thus arose from the fact that, in the first few years after being privatized, the companies were allowed to continue making supernormal profits, or **monopoly economic rent**.

Contestable markets

In 1998 the government announced that it was strengthening competition policy in Britain with a new Competition Bill, giving new powers and a 20 per cent increase in resources to the **Office of Fair Trading** (OFT). Under the new arrangements, the OFT will have the right to fine firms up to 10 per cent of their turnover for abusing their competitive positions.

During 1998 and 1999, the OFT carried out reviews of the supermarket sector, following claims that the four biggest supermarkets – Sainsbury, Tesco, Safeway and Asda – were taking advantage of their market power. It also examined the pricing of new cars in Britain, in response to persistent claims that these prices were significantly higher than in other EU countries.

The government's approach – along with its regulatory framework for the privatized utilities (who were charged a £5 billion, one-off, windfall tax on their excess profits in 1997) – is based on the theory of **contestable markets**. The task of the OFT, with the **Competition Commission** (formerly the Monopolies and Mergers Commission or MMC) and the **Restrictive Practices Court**, should be to ensure contestable markets.

Thus the best way to ensure competition, a better deal for consumers and greater efficiency is not to seek to break up monopolies through anti-trust laws. Instead, the emphasis is upon ensuring that **barriers to entry** come down, so that new firms can compete and prices fall.

As well as the domestic dimension of this approach, it also has an international aspect, in the encouragement of global free trade through the World Trade Organization (WTO). *Faced with new competition, inefficient firms will have no place to hide.*

Does competition increase productivity?

According to the Treasury, it does:

> '*A key part of the government's productivity strategy must be to ensure that robust competition in product markets thrives, over time driving productivity improvements towards world-class levels, and that there is a sufficiently strong competition regime to ensure that it does.*'

Interestingly, this was not always thought to be the case. One of the reasons for the strength of Japanese industry, for example, was traditionally thought to be that it had the benefit of a large, and protected, home market.

Japan makes an interesting case study. While its manufacturing sector, heavily engaged in export markets, was highly productive, the Japanese economy had low productivity across other, mainly domestic, sectors of the economy, including farming and service-sector activities such as retailing. These sectors mopped up much of the workforce, giving Japan low unemployment alongside industrial success.

Economists would always tend to regard competition as a good thing. Businessmen, however, may see it differently. While economists would expect the spur of greater competition to encourage firms to invest in productivity-enhancing equipment and methods, it is possible to envisage companies responding differently. They might see competition, and the threat of losing market share, as a reason to scale down investment plans. *Which of these two motivations dominates will determine whether a strategy to boost competition will raise productivity.*

KEY WORDS

Productivity	Comparative advantage
GDP per capita	Perfect competition
Living standards	Monopoly
Value added	Monopoly economic rent
Capital productivity	Office of Fair Trading
Total factor productivity	Contestable markets
Economies of scale	Competition Commission
Innovation	Restrictive Practices Court
Competitiveness	Barriers to entry

Reading list

Atkinson, B., Baker, P. and Milward, R., Chapter 3 in *Economic Policy*, Macmillan, 1996.

Ball, J., Chapter 3 in *The British Economy at the Crossroads*, FT/Pitman, 1998.

Buxton, T., Chapman, P. and Temple, P., Chapter 17 in *Britain's Economic Performance*, 2nd edn, Routledge, 1998.

Maunder, P., Myers, D., Wall, N. and Miller, R., Chapter 27 in *Economics Explained*, 3rd edn, Collins Educational, 1995.

Useful website

DTI: www.dti.gov.uk/

Essay topics

1. Do you agree with the view that specialization and competition should be extended to all areas of the economy, both internal and international? [40 marks] [University of Cambridge Local Examinations Syndicate 1997]
2. (a) Distinguish between production and productivity. [10 marks]
   (b) Evaluate *two* policies a government could introduce to increase productivity. [15 marks]

Data response question

This task is based on a question set by the University of Oxford Delegacy of Local Examinations in 1998. Read the piece below and study the table. In answering the questions that follow you should use not only the information given, but also your own knowledge of economics, economic analysis and economic institutions.

Competition policy

Adam Smith said that 'the division of labour is limited by the extent of the market'. By this he meant that the ability of firms to enjoy increased economies of scale was dependent upon their ability to expand their sales. Firms benefiting from economies of scale will acquire a competitive advantage over smaller firms. This process will result in industries being characterized by larger, and therefore fewer, firms. Monopoly power may be the result.

Table A gives the proportion of output and employment provided by the five largest firms in various industries. It gives some idea of the industries in which economies of scale are most important, and the market power enjoyed by these firms.

This poses a problem for government. If large size increases economic efficiency, then monopolies may be justified as being a necessary consequence of larger sized firms. Any attempt by government to enforce competition might reduce the ability of firms to enjoy economies of scale, and so harm their efficiency.

Competition policy then becomes a matter of trading off the efficiency gains of large size against the possible abuses of monopoly power which could lead to a loss of economic welfare for consumers. Given the difficulties in assessing *supernormal profits*, it becomes very difficult to judge whether monopoly power benefits or harms the economy.

When we consider the international sphere there are further implications. Free trade will permit firms to expand their markets overseas. This will promote economies of scale and so increase

Table A Five firm concentration ratios in various UK industries, 1992

Industry	Number of enterprises in the industry	Employment provided by the five largest enterprises (%)	Gross output provided by the five largest enterprises (%)
Iron and steel	27	90.9	95.3
Bolts, nuts, etc.	1888	9.6	11.4
Hand tools	8281	8.4	15.1
Motor vehicles	185	80.4	82.9
Tobacco	22	97.7	99.5
Processing of plastics	4461	6.8	8.8
Leather goods	797	12.4	16.2

Source: ONS, *Annual Census of Production 1992*, © Crown Copyright 1992

efficiency. Hence one possible consequence of the single European market will be the encouragement of monopoly power by encouraging the growth of firms.

If this growth of firms leads to increased numbers of monopoly and oligopoly markets, prices will become less and less flexible. Macroeconomic theory places considerable emphasis on falling prices as a way of relieving a lack of demand in the economy. With monopolies and oligopolies this process becomes more difficult.

1. (a) Explain *three* possible sources of economies of scale. [8 marks]
   (b) Explain the link between competition and the ability to earn 'supernormal profits'. [8 marks]
   (c) Why might 'the single European market' encourage the growth of monopoly power? [8 marks]
2. (a) Identify reasons for the different degrees of industrial concentration shown in Table A. [12 marks]
   (b) To what extent do the data in the table give information on the degree of monopoly power in the industries listed? What other information might be useful? [12 marks]
3. If larger firms can achieve lower average costs of production, does this always increase economic efficiency? [16 marks]
4. Assess how a fall in the general price level affects aggregate demand. [16 marks]

Chapter Eight

Devolution and regional policy

'*We believe it is right to decentralize power, to open up government, to reform parliament and to increase individual rights. The elements of our programme are well known:*

- *a Welsh Assembly and a Scottish Parliament giving the people of Wales and Scotland more control over their own affairs within the United Kingdom*
- *an elected Mayor and new strategic authority for London with more accountability in the regions of England*
- *new rights for citizens with the incorporation into UK law of the European Convention on Human Rights*
- *freedom of information*
- *a referendum on the voting system for the House of Commons.*'

Tony Blair, July 1997

Why regional policy?

Just as part of the aim of taxation policy is to achieve a more equitable distribution of income, so regional policy aims to bring about a more even spread of economic activity, and in particular employment, between different regions. There is also, as the quote from Tony Blair at the head of this chapter illustrates, a powerful political dimension to policy towards the regions. If large areas of the country believe they are being given a raw deal by Westminster, they will react against the incumbent government.

The UK is characterized by an uneven distribution of economic activity.

- The south-east of England covers only 11 per cent of the UK's land area but accounts for about 30 per cent of the population and generates 36 per cent of GDP. GDP per head in the South East is about 120 per cent of the national average. House prices are significantly higher in the southern regions.
- Five regions – the South East, the South West, East Anglia, the East Midlands and the West Midlands – together cover 38 per cent of the UK's land area but house 58 per cent of its population and are responsible for more than 62 per cent of GDP.

- Typically, unemployment has been significantly higher in the north of England, Wales, Scotland and Northern Ireland than in those more southerly areas.

Figure 24 shows the way the UK is divided for the purpose of regional comparisons, and Table 3 shows the sharp regional differences in GDP per head. GDP per head in London, for example, is nearly 25 per cent above the national average, while GDP per head in Northern Ireland is almost 20 per cent below that average.

Regional policy grew up as essentially an element of employment policy (particularly in the post-1945 period) because wide variations in unemployment between regions would have made it difficult to achieve national full employment.

But regional policy is also linked to other objectives, including promoting growth and maintaining low inflation. Either goal is made more difficult if certain regions have an over-concentration of activity while others have of permanently under-used capacity.

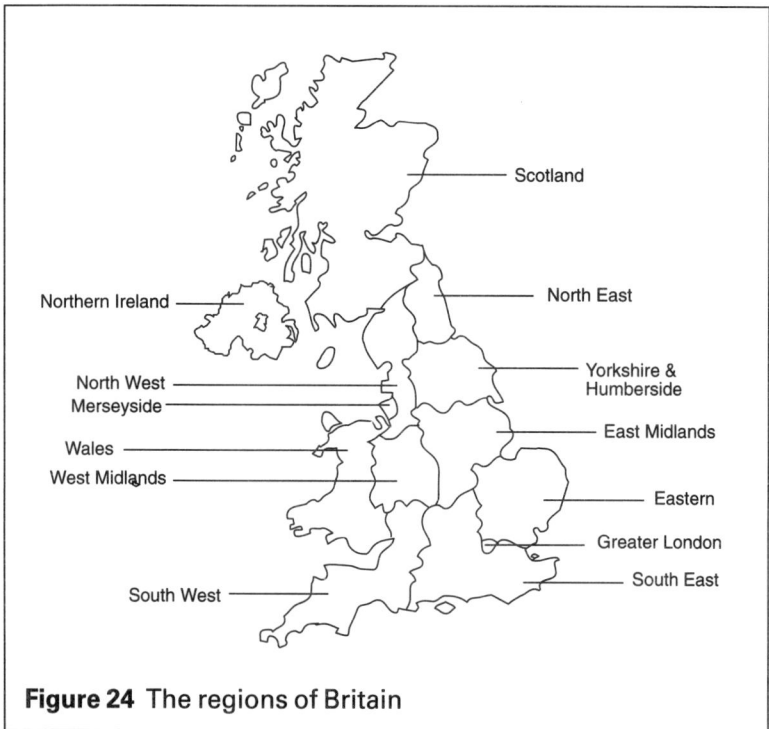

Figure 24 The regions of Britain

Table 3 GDP per head and unemployment by region of the UK

	GDP per head (1996 = 100)	Unemployment rate (%)
North East	84.3	8.8
North West and Merseyside	90.9	6.0
Yorkshire and Humberside	89.5	6.7
East Midlands	94.3	5.0
West Midlands	93.5	6.5
Eastern	108.8	4.5
London	123.3	7.6
South East	114.5	4.3
South West	94.7	4.7
England	101.7	5.9
Wales	83.1	7.1
Scotland	99.1	7.6
Northern Ireland	81.2	7.6
UK	100.0	6.2

The unemployment rate is the Labour Force Survey (LFS) measure for September–November 1998.

Source: Labour Force Survey, ONS © Crown Copyright 1999

The regional problem

Economists have identified three main types of regional economic problem:

- An **underdeveloped region** has never been a favoured location for industry, and has suffered from a decline in agriculture, the traditional source of employment. Parts of West Wales, rural areas of Scotland and Devon and Cornwall could fit into this category.
- A **depressed region** once had a significant industrial base, but has suffered from the decline of key industries. Traditional industrial areas of the north of England and of Scotland, once reliant on steel, coal or shipbuilding, have at various times been depressed regions.
- A **congested region,** into which too much activity is concentrated, results in congestion costs, from overcrowded roads to wage pressures resulting from labour shortages and a decline in the quality of life arising from insufficient open spaces. The south-east of England and, for much of the post-war period, the West Midlands, were regarded as congested regions.

Two sets of factors determine which category a region is likely to fall into.

- The first are **locational,** where a region's location puts it at a disadvantage, because it is too far away from main markets, or because transport links are poor.
- The second are **structural,** where the structure of a region's economy acts as a disadvantage. Thus, when manufacturing industry experienced a third downturn in the space of two decades in the late 1990s, it was the West Midlands and northern regions of England which were most affected, the diversified regional economy of the South East, with its wide range of industries and services, least so.

Regional policy can be designed to act on both sets of factors. A way of alleviating locational problems, for example, would be to improve transport links, while a deliberate strategy of attracting new industries to an area can be used to compensate for structural problems.

The recent history of South Wales shows how regional policy has been brought to bear on both sets of problems. The extension of the M4 motorway and the building of the first Severn Bridge helped overcome the area's locational disadvantages; while new light industries, such as electronics, were given incentives to come to South Wales and replace declining coal and steel industries.

The rise of regional policy

In the 1950s and 60s, regional policy was regarded as an essential tool for governments wishing to maintain full employment.

The idea of the **regional multiplier,** whereby help for one region would spill over into additional demand in other regions, was popular. A policy which boosted output and cut unemployment in a region operating below capacity would be more likely to result in beneficial multiplier effects throughout the rest of the economy.

On the other hand, an increase in demand in an already congested region, perhaps through a national tax cut, could have an adverse effect, by creating inflationary pressures and the risk that the additional demand would merely result in a disproportionate rise in imports.

Regional policy operated in two broad ways:

- The first was through policies to encourage a shift of activity to depressed areas.
- The second was to provide people in those areas with an incentive to move to where the work was – to increase the **geographical mobility of labour.**

Though geographical mobility of labour is considered to be a good thing, as discussed in the next chapter, the first approach was favoured. By encouraging people in depressed areas to move to already congested regions, the former would risk losing their most talented and educated people, while the latter would become even more congested.

Within these two broad approaches, governments offered both the 'carrot' of incentives, and the 'stick' of preventing development in certain areas.

Examples of the former included **regional development grants** and other incentives for firms to locate in depressed areas. The latter included **industrial development certificates** and, for a period, **office development certificates**, used to prevent further development in congested areas such as the South East and the West Midlands.

In the area of encouraging workers to move to where the work was, the government provided assistance with transport costs and, for people moving from depressed areas, a weekly grant for a period to top-up their earnings.

Regional policy achieved some of its aims. Over the period 1945–81 the South East lost 1647 manufacturing establishments, and the West Midlands 334, a total of 1981 firms, while the rest of the country gained 1706. Successful though this shows regional policy to have been, it would have been more beneficial had the relocation occurred in service-sector employment. Another estimate, by the Department of Trade and Industry, suggested 784 000 jobs were created in assisted areas between 1960 and 1981 as a result of regional policy.

The fall of regional policy

Despite the apparent successes of regional policy outlined above, the Conservative government elected in 1979 embarked on a rundown of regional policy, for two main reasons.

- Firstly, it believed that businesses, and not the government, were best able to decide where they should locate, and that industrial development certificates and similar restrictions interfered with such decisions. The fear was that, instead of directing investment elsewhere in the country, it could prevent it altogether.
- Secondly, the Conservative government was committed to reducing public spending, and believed regional development grants and other government incentives were a wasteful use of public funds.

Within this approach, the government also identified regional problems as more localized than in the past. Instead of targeting entire regions, much smaller areas were selected. **Enterprise zones**, offering companies 100 per cent capital allowances on investment in the first year (they could offset all their investment against tax), exemption from local authority rates and development land tax, and freedom from certain government controls and bureaucracy, were created in 25 of these smaller areas during the 1980s.

Nor were all the areas selected for assistance in the traditionally depressed regions. When the government redrew the map of assisted areas in the early 1990s, not only did it significantly scale down the coverage of regional policy, but it also included parts of London (Park Royal and the Lea Valley), and the rest of the South East (Clacton, Dover, Folkestone, Hastings, the Isle of Wight and Sittingbourne) as eligible for assistance.

Devolution

In September 1997, referendums were held in Scotland and Wales on the establishment of a **Scottish Parliament** and a **Welsh Assembly**. Both were passed, although only narrowly in the case of Wales. The effect will be to increase significantly the regional political and economic autonomy of Scotland and Wales.

In Scotland, following elections in May 1999, the 129-member Parliament, operating under a First Minister and an Executive of ministers, assumed powers for health, education, local government, housing, planning, tourism, police and fire services, economic development, financial support for industry, the law, and other matters. Westminster retained control of constitutional matters, defence, foreign affairs, most economic and financial matters, social security, competition and consumer protection policy, and other 'national' issues.

Significantly, the Scottish Parliament was given the power to vary the basic rate of income tax – either up or down – by up to three pence in the pound, using the proceeds to increase public spending in Scotland, in the case of a rise in tax, or cutting the rate of tax to cut spending.

In the case of Wales, the Assembly – also operating under a First Minister and Executive – assumed responsibility for the £7 billion annual Welsh Office budget and thus took responsibility for health, education, environmental matters, and the other broad policy areas similarly devolved to the Scottish Parliament. Unlike in Scotland, however, the Assembly has no powers to vary income tax.

Devolution has led to demands from the English regions for greater autonomy. In February 1999, the Labour government announced that it was considering reviving the Standing Committee on Regional Affairs, which had last sat in 1978. **Regional Development Agencies**

SNP to put up taxes by 1p

CHRIS DEERIN

The SNP plan to make Scots pay 1p more in income tax than the rest of Britain. Chancellor Gordon Brown promised in his budget to cut the basic rate of income tax from 23p to 22p next April. But today, SNP Treasury spokesman John Swinney will reveal the Nats' plan to keep the tax rate at 23p, raising £230 million for the Scottish Parliament. He will pledge to use the money for public services. The cash will be ring-fenced for health, education and housing.

The move is a high-risk strategy for the SNP, who are relying on Scots being willing to pay more tax than the rest of the UK. It will lead to accusations that an independent Scotland will mean a far higher tax burden...

The SNP believe their plan will not come as a heavy blow to voters because, rather than paying more, Scots will simply not receive the 1p tax cut next April. An SNP spokeman said 'Labour turned their gaze away from us in their attempts to woo middle England, but polling shows that Scots believe in funding their public services'...

The SNP decision has been taken after top-level talks and number-crunching following the Chancellor's give-away budget. Although the move will have to be ratified at the SNP's annual conference this week, the Nats clearly believe they have grabbed the moral high ground.

But last night, Scottish Labour could hardly contain their delight at what they saw as a major miscalculation. They said it proved that the Nats were a 'tax-and-spend' party and that only Labour were fit and ready to govern Scotland. A spokeswoman said: 'There is now a clear choice in May between Labour's devolution plans of a cut in tax and more money into health, education and jobs – all priorities for the Scottish people – or the SNP's divorce plans for hikes in tax and poorer public services alongside more and more businesses being devastated and jobs being driven away'... They may well have got to the point where they are trying to justify increasing tax, but they are failing to acknowledge what this Labour government is doing in terms of investment. ...

Adapted from the *Scottish Daily Record*, 12 March 1999

are to take on the role of setting strategies for each region. They will manage the government's **Single Regeneration Budget** which will aim to launch major job-creating projects in the most deprived local authority areas.

Despite this, it does not appear that regional policy will revert to its former levels. Although devolution gives Scotland and Wales greater control over their affairs, it does not imply an increase in resources – although the Scottish Parliament could vote itself an increase by increasing income tax.

The economics of independence

In the case of Scotland, if not Wales, many observers see devolution as a stepping-stone towards full independence, as is the policy aim of the Scottish National Party (SNP). An independent Scotland, it is argued, could run its own economic affairs, and adopt a separate currency or join the euro ahead of any decision to do so by the British government.

Scotland, with a population of five million, is certainly not too small an economic unit to prosper within the EU – there are smaller EU member states. One central argument, however, is the extent to which Scotland is currently supported by the rest of the UK.

Table 4 shows Treasury data for government expenditure per head by region. Scotland has government expenditure per head of nearly £1000 more than England, and nearly £1700 more than the lowest English region, the South East (although note that London is high because of the concentration of civil service activity in the capital). Wales is also well above the English average, Northern Ireland even more so, partly because of high levels of security expenditure.

Table 4 Identifiable government expenditure per head, 1995/96 (£)

North West	3578
North East	3814
Yorkshire and Humberside	3322
East Midlands	3101
West Midlands	3278
South West	3144
Eastern	2999
London	4228
South East	2974
England	3754
Scotland	4682
Wales	4452
Northern Ireland	5211
United Kingdom	3911

Source: HM Treasury, Public Expenditure Statistical Analyses 1998–99.

Scotland has higher government expenditure per head because, for example, the population is spread out over a wide area, making the delivery of public services more expensive. The argument this provides *against* devolution is that, if these costs had to be financed by Scottish taxpayers alone, the tax burden in Scotland would rise sharply relative to the rest of the UK, providing an incentive for businesses and individuals to relocate to England.

This argument is, however, strongly challenged by the SNP. It suggests that, far from being subsidised by the rest of the UK, Scotland had a budget surplus with the rest of the UK of £91 billion over the period 1979–94. The figure was arrived at largely by allocating 90 per cent of North Sea oil revenues to Scotland. The argument over the costs and benefits of independence are likely to feature strongly in the policy debate in the coming years.

Three reports published during the run-up to the May 1999 elections to the Scottish Parliament, by the David Hume Institute, the Pieda economic consultancy and the Centre for Economics and Business Research, concluded that an independent Scotland would face a 'negative dowry' – a gap between public spending and taxation – arising from the loss of the UK subsidy (i.e. the fact that public expenditure per head is higher in Scotland). This would require, they said, either a reduction in public spending or higher taxation.

All three reports concluded, however, that the success of an independent Scotland over the longer-term would depend on the ability of politicians to adopt supply-side economic policies that were friendly towards the creation of new businesses and jobs. Within the UK, Scotland's modern record on both counts has been mixed.

KEY WORDS

Underdeveloped region	Industrial development
Depressed region	certificates
Congested region	Office development certificates
Locational factors	Enterprise zones
Structural factors	Scottish Parliament
Regional multiplier	Welsh Assembly
Geographical mobility of	Regional Development
labour	Agencies
Regional development grants	Single Regeneration Budget

Reading list

Atkinson, B., Baker, P. and Milward, R., Chapter 7 in *Economic Policy*, Macmillan, 1996.

Griffiths, A. and Wall, S., Chapter 21 in *Applied Economics*, 7th edn, Addison-Wesley Longman, 1997.

Hill, B., Chapter 5 in *The European Union*, 3rd edn, Heinemann Educational, 1998.
Sloman, J., Chapter 22 in *Economics*, 3rd edn, Prentice Hall, 1997.
Smith, D., *North and South*, Penguin, 1994.

Essay topics

1. (a) Why are some regions in the UK poorer than others? [10 marks]
   (b) Assess the risks of the UK becoming one of the poor regions of the European Union. [15 marks]
2. Discuss the implications for the UK economy of Scottish and Welsh devolution. [25 marks]

Useful websites

Scottish Office: www.scotland.gov.uk/
Scottish National Party: www.snp.org.uk/

Data response question

This task is based on a question set by the University of Cambridge Local Examinations Syndicate in 1996. Read the following piece and study the charts. Then answer all the questions that follow.

The changing pattern of employment in the UK

Since 1980 there has been a considerable change in the pattern of employment in the UK economy with several leading economists expressing concern about the UK's manufacturing sector. There has been much interest in the growth of women's employment, and concern that women's part-time jobs may be replacing full-time jobs for men. The accompanying four charts are adapted from data issued by the Department of Employment.

1. (a) Compare the trends in manufacturing and non-manufacturing employment during the period. [1 mark]
   (b) Discuss *two* possible economic consequences of this change in the pattern of employment. [4 marks]
2. (a) What happened to labour productivity in manufacturing industries between 1983 and 1990? Using the data, explain your reasoning. [2 marks]
   (b) Give *two* possible causes of changes in labour productivity. [2 marks]

3. To what extent does the information in Figure B support the view that women's part-time jobs are replacing male full-time jobs? [5 marks]
4. Assuming no increase in the level of population, discuss whether the data indicate an increase in the standard of living between 1983 and 1993. [6 marks]

Figure A Manufacturing and non-manufacturing employees in employment in the UK (seasonally adjusted)

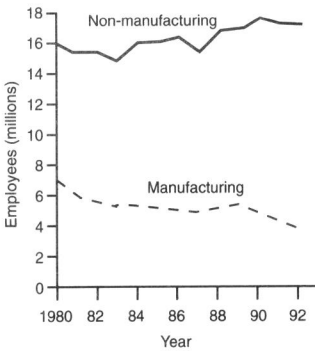

Figure B Shares of total employment (UK)

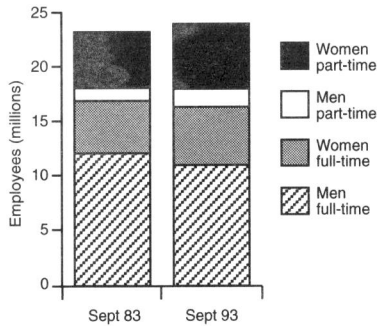

Figure C Output of UK manufacturing industries (1985 = 100)

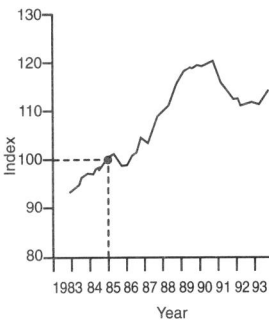

Figure D GDP (1985 = 100)

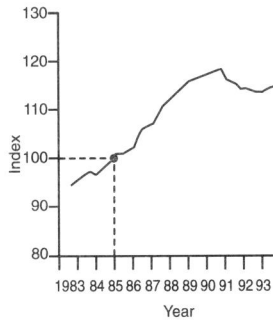

Chapter Nine

Britain, Europe and the euro

'*The government believes that British membership of a successful single currency would benefit Britain. Provided the economic benefits are clear and unambiguous, Britain should join.*'
Financial Statement and Budget Report, HM Treasury, March 1998

The UK and the European Union

The history of the modern **European Union** (EU) dates back to the early 1950s when six European countries – France, Germany, Belgium, the Netherlands, Luxembourg and Italy – signed the Treaty of Paris of 1951, establishing the **European Coal and Steel Community** (ECSC), which provided for co-operation in these industries. Britain was invited to take part in the initial discussions but declined to join.

Six years later, in 1957, the **Treaty of Rome** was signed by the Six, this time bringing into being the **European Economic Community** (EEC) – another treaty was signed at the same time establishing Euratom, the European Atomic Energy Community. Britain, again, did not join, preferring instead to forge a separate free trade area, the **European Free Trade Association** (EFTA), along with Austria, Denmark, Norway, Portugal, Sweden and Switzerland, in 1960.

Within the EEC, the **Common Agricultural Policy** (CAP), providing a wide-ranging, and costly, system of price support for farm produce was introduced in 1962. By 1968, after progressive reductions in internal tariffs, and the convergence by the Six around a **common external tariff**, the EEC had become a **customs union**.

The UK first applied for membership of the EEC in 1961 but was rejected on two occasions, in 1963 and 1967, largely because of the opposition of the then French president, General de Gaulle. Britain finally joined, on 1 January 1973, along with Denmark and Ireland.

Further enlargements took place in 1981 (Greece), 1986 (Spain and Portugal), and 1995 (Austria, Finland and Sweden), making 15 members in all.

During the 1980s, with Margaret Thatcher as British Prime Minister, much European Community business was taken up with the issue of Britain's contribution to the budget – she successfully won a rebate at Fontainebleau in 1984. Britain was also influential in pushing for the

Single European Act of 1987, which established the European single market at the beginning of 1993, and thus Europe started on the road to becoming a common market.

Britain was less enthusiastic about the Treaty on European Union, agreed at Maastricht in December 1991, which provided for European economic and monetary union (EMU) as well as closer co-operation on other matters, notably social policy, including workers' rights. John Major, as Prime Minister, secured the right of the UK to opt-in to both EMU and the so-called social protocol on workers' rights at a time of the government's choosing. Under the Maastricht treaty, the European Communities (the combined name for the EEC, ECSC and Euratom) became the European Union.

Customs unions and common markets

The EEC was popularly known as the Common Market from its inception in the 1950s. It was, however, more correctly described as a customs union, defined as an area with a common external tariff (i.e. goods entering the area would face the same tariff or other restriction no matter which country they entered).

The second requirement of a customs union is that there be no internal tariffs on trade. A customs union was thus achieved for the original six EEC members by the late 1960s.

A common market is more ambitious. It means a free market within the area in goods, services, capital and people – no restrictions on the ability of individuals to live and work elsewhere in the area. The move to establish a true common market in Europe began with the Single European Act.

Is a customs union and/or a common market a good thing? Both represent a *limited* free trade area, rather than universal free trade. Economists define two effects from the creation of a customs union and its evolution into a common market:

- The first is trade creation – lowering internal trade barriers within the EU has led to increased trade between member countries.
- The second is trade diversion – the preferential treatment accorded to trade between member countries diverts trade away from other countries.

The common external tariff, in other words, can be expected to result in a fall-off in imports from outside the EU. If this tariff is set at a high level, then it is possible that, for consumers, the negative effects of trade diversion could outweigh the positive impact of trade creation.

Economists agree that universal free trade is better than limited free trade. The latter is known as a **second-best solution.**

The effects of both trade creation and trade diversion can be seen clearly in the statistics. Nearly 60 per cent of the external trade of

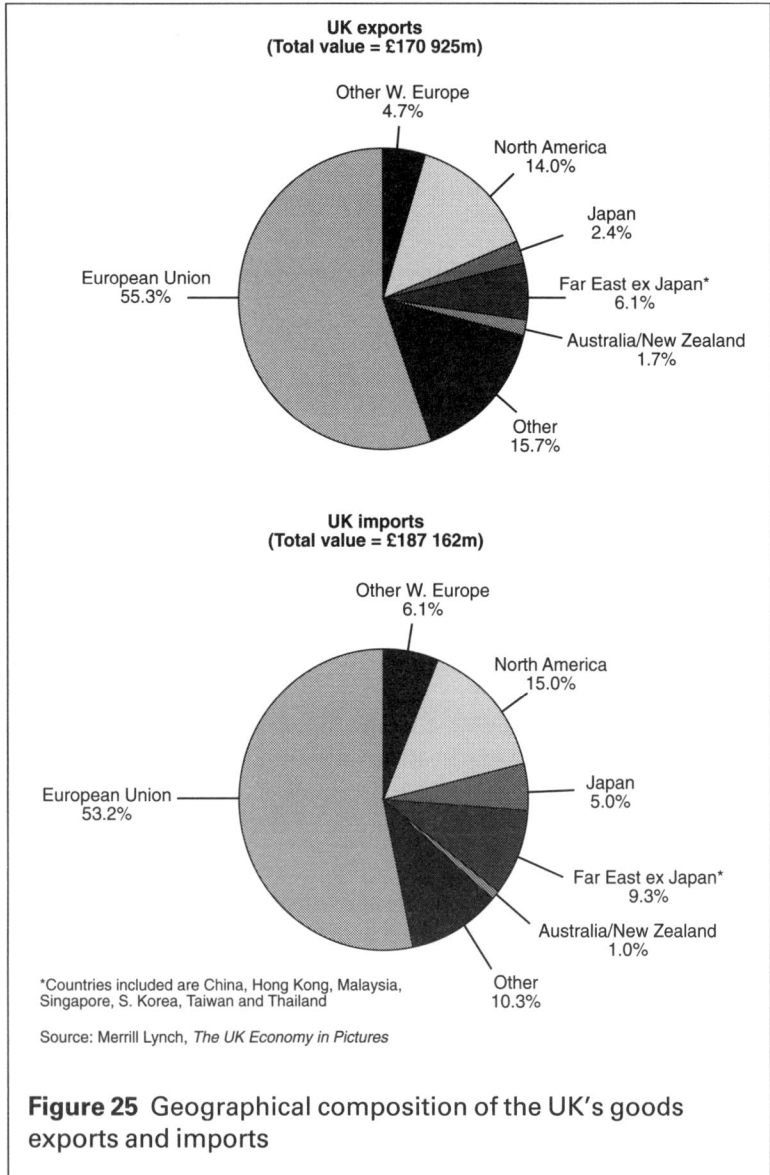

UK exports
(Total value = £170 925m)

Other W. Europe
4.7%

North America
14.0%

Japan
2.4%

Far East ex Japan*
6.1%

Australia/New Zealand
1.7%

Other
15.7%

European Union
55.3%

UK imports
(Total value = £187 162m)

Other W. Europe
6.1%

North America
15.0%

Japan
5.0%

Far East ex Japan*
9.3%

Australia/New Zealand
1.0%

Other
10.3%

European Union
53.2%

*Countries included are China, Hong Kong, Malaysia, Singapore, S. Korea, Taiwan and Thailand

Source: Merrill Lynch, *The UK Economy in Pictures*

Figure 25 Geographical composition of the UK's goods exports and imports

members of the EU is, on average, with other member countries, a figure which rises to more than 75 per cent in the case of Belgium and Luxembourg. In 1958 about a quarter of Britain's external trade was with the other 14 members of the current EU. Trade with the Commonwealth and with the USA was, in overall terms, much more important. By 1980, after membership, this had risen to more than 40 per cent. The recent position, with more than 55 per cent of export and import trade with other EU countries, is shown in Figure 25.

European economic and monetary union

From the very start of the post-war process of European integration, indeed on occasions in more distant history, politicians have seen the creation of a single currency for Europe – of economic and monetary union – as a central goal. While countries can enter and leave customs unions, common markets and other such arrangements, a single currency was always regarded as a binding form of integration, which would permanently unite member states, although not everybody agrees that the single currency will achieve this.

In 1969, at a summit in The Hague, leaders of the six EEC countries agreed to adopt the goal of achieving monetary union. In 1970, the **Werner committee**, under the chairmanship of Pierre Werner, the Luxembourg Prime Minister, proposed a timetable for achieving monetary union by 1980 and this was adopted by European leaders. However, events in international financial markets, including the collapse of the post-war **Bretton Woods** system of fixed-but-adjustable exchange rates, and the economic crisis caused by the first Organization of Petroleum Exporting Countries' (OPEC) oil price hike, led to this timetable being abandoned.

Hopes of closer monetary integration were not, however, abandoned. In 1979, the **European Monetary System** came into being. The main element of this was the **exchange rate mechanism,** or ERM. The ERM was a mechanism for ensuring currency stability in Europe, with currencies allowed to fluctuate only modestly – by 2.25 per cent or 6 per cent – on either side of a central rate, determined in terms of the **European Currency Unit** (the ecu), the 'basket' currency of the then EEC. Britain did not join at the outset, although the other eight members did.

The ERM had a mixed record. In its first eight years there were 11 significant currency realignments, and the aim of its founders to create a zone of monetary stability could not be said to have been achieved.

Britain, the ERM and 'Black Wednesday'

Britain finally joined the ERM in October 1990. The pound sterling was allowed a 6 per cent margin of fluctuation around a central rate against the ecu, or a rate of 2.95 German marks (deutsch marks).

Entry into the ERM was seen as stabilizing the pound on a permanent basis. John Major, Chancellor of the Exchequer at the time of entry and Prime Minister shortly afterwards, said membership of the ERM meant 'the soft option, the devaluer's option' would be no more. It was also a means of reducing Britain's then high interest rates to European levels. Interest rates were reduced from 15 per cent to 14 per cent on entry, and progressively reduced to 10 per cent in succeeding months.

Britain, however, was entering a serious recession at the time of entry and, far from providing the means of escaping it, the ERM was seen to be locking Britain into too high an exchange rate and interest rates. Less than two years later, on 'Black Wednesday', 16 September 1992, the strains grew too much and Britain was forced out of the ERM by a massive wave of selling of the pound. Once outside the ERM, the government reduced interest rates sharply, to 6 per cent, and set in train the policies that were eventually to lead to Bank of England

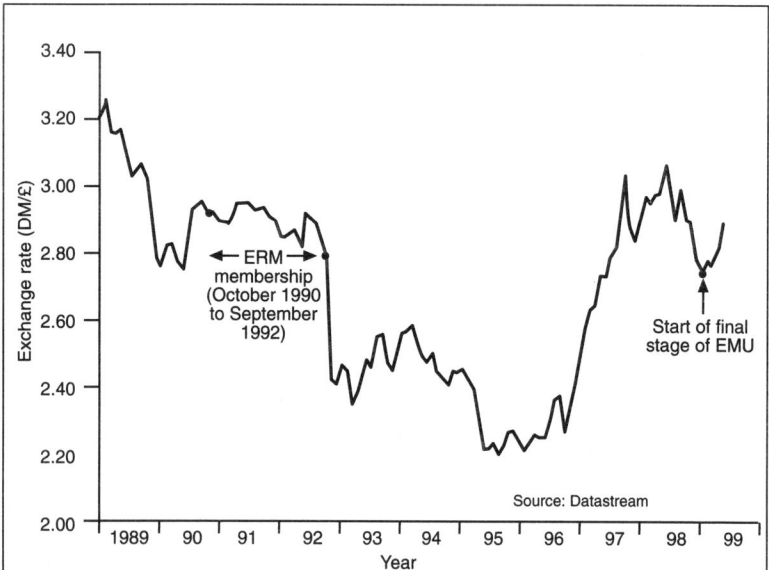

Figure 26 Sterling against the DM, before and after ERM membership

independence. Figure 26 shows how the pound fluctuated before and after membership of the ERM.

The episode coloured British attitudes to European economic and monetary union. It also nearly precipitated the collapse of the ERM. Italy dropped out at the same time as Britain. The following summer, in July/August 1993, the ERM came under intense pressure following heavy selling of the French franc. Only by adopting a very wide currency exchange band (15 per cent) was the crisis averted. Had the ERM collapsed, it is likely the drive towards a single currency would have been halted.

Achieving EMU

The EU's second big drive towards EMU came after the signing of the Single European Act in 1986. The preamble to the Act included a restatement of the goal of achieving EMU.

Following this, a committee of central bankers and experts, under the chairmanship of Jacques Delors, the then president of the European Commission, investigated the practicalities of EMU. The **Delors report** was published in 1989.

Two years later, at Maastricht in the Netherlands, a timetable for EMU was agreed, with all member countries except Britain and Denmark agreeing to participate. (At that time Austria, Finland and Sweden were not part of the EU; they joined in 1995.) Britain and Denmark have EMU 'opt-outs' – or rather the right to opt in to EMU at a time of their choosing.

The Maastricht timetable was set as follows:

- *Stage 1:* All participating countries were to be members of the ERM and to be observing its normal fluctuation margins prior to the start of the second stage.
- *Stage 2:* On 1 January 1994, the European Monetary Institute (the European Central Bank's forerunner) would come into being and oversee countries' preparations for EMU.
- *Stage 3:* The third and final stage, including the changeover from national notes and coins to the single currency (which acquired its name, the **euro**, in 1995), would begin on 1 January 1997 if a majority of countries were ready, or by 1 January 1999 at the latest.

As it turned out, 1 January 1999 marked the euro's start as an *electronic or commercial currency* for 11 countries – Austria, Belgium, Finland, France, Germany, Ireland, Italy, Luxembourg, the Netherlands, Portugal and Spain – with the changeover to the euro from national notes and coins scheduled for the first half of 2002. To qualify for EMU, countries had to meet the so-called **Maastricht criteria** for the reference year of 1997 (see the boxed item).

Maastricht criteria

The criteria, which also apply to future EMU entrants, are:

- an inflation rate of not more than 1.5 percentage points above the average of the three member states with the lowest inflation rates
- a long-term interest rate within 2 percentage points of the average of the three members with the best inflation performance
- a maximum budget deficit, including central, regional, local government and social security funds, of 3 per cent of GDP
- a public debt ratio of less than 60 per cent of GDP
- a currency which for two years has observed the normal fluctuation bands of the ERM.

The pros and cons of EMU

EMU generates a great deal of political heat, particularly in Britain, where opponents see it as leading to a loss of sovereignty and resulting, inevitably, in full political union.

Eurosceptics have deep suspicions about the 'economic' in 'economic and monetary union'. While some see this as merely representing the existing single market, others see it as implying harmonization of all taxes, labour laws and other aspects of the economic environment, even the eventual creation of a powerful European 'Treasury' as a fiscal policy counterweight to the European Central Bank.

Leaving this debate aside, what are the *economic* advantages and disadvantages of monetary union?

Advantages
The advantages are as follows:

- Companies and individuals would save on **transaction costs** within the EMU area because the need to change currencies would be eliminated. On one calculation, a traveller starting with £100 in Britain and moving around Europe, simply changing the money for local currency in each of the EU member states, would be left with £50 or less on their return. Transaction cost savings are also important for business. They have been estimated to be worth 0.3–0.4 per cent of the EU's combined gross 'domestic' product.
- Exchange rate uncertainty would be eliminated in the euro area,

making it easier for businesses to plan and price. A common problem for British business has been that the pound has shifted sharply, either making it difficult for them to export (the strong pound problem) or pushing up the cost of their imported materials and components (the weak pound problem).

- The opportunities to exploit the European single market would increase. Some see national currencies as 'the final barrier to trade'. With a single currency, it is argued, Europe would be able to exploit fully the economies of scale and other advantages of a large single market, and rival the USA in economic terms.

Others see additional advantages. The absence of the devaluation weapon, it is argued, would force companies, indeed whole economies, to become more competitive. Traditional high-inflation countries in the EU, such as Italy and Spain, have seen a big advantage in EMU because it enables them, under the auspices of the European Central Bank, to achieve low, German-style inflation. Britain could benefit from this. Inflation and interest rates have tended to be lower in countries such as Germany, Austria and the Netherlands, than in Britain.

Disadvantages
There are, however, also significant potential disadvantages associated with EMU.

The main doubt concerns the problem of having a single monetary policy for the whole of a very large area. This is sometimes known as the 'one size fits all' problem.

Think of it in terms of Britain. When the economy of the south-east of England is booming but the rest of the country is struggling, the onus is on the Bank of England to raise interest rates to head off inflationary pressures in the south-east, even if this would further depress other parts of the country. It would be better, but impossible, if different rates of interest were available for different regions. In EMU, this problem is writ large. Can the same interest rate be suited to conditions across 11 different countries, without causing severe problems?

One reason why the difficulty could arise is that different countries are insufficiently 'converged'. The Maastricht criteria ensured financial and fiscal convergence but not *real* economic convergence (measured by unemployment rates and, for example, whether different member states are at similar stages in the economic cycle).

In 1961 an economist called Robert Mundell wrote a paper on the subject of **optimum currency areas**. He argued that three things were needed for an optimum currency area:

- Workers had to be prepared and able to move between regions/countries in response to high unemployment where they were living and job opportunities elsewhere. They had to be 'geographically mobile'.
- Wages had to be flexible – falling wages in high unemployment areas encouraging companies within the currency area to locate there.
- There had to be scope for sufficient 'fiscal transfers' – that is by means of taxation and public spending – between parts of the currency area to offset problems.

The USA satisfies these conditions, and can be said to be an optimum currency area. Europe does not at present, although advocates of EMU would say these conditions could develop over time.

Britain and the euro

In October 1997, the Labour government announced that it was in favour in principle of joining the euro but that it would be not do so in the 'first wave' in January 1999. A decision to join, it said, would be a three-way decision – supported by government, parliament and the public, in a referendum. No decision would be taken, it said, until the following parliament.

To join EMU, Britain would necessarily have to meet the five Maastricht criteria. In addition, the Chancellor set out five specifically British 'economic tests'. These were:

- Would joining EMU create better conditions for firms making long-term decisions to invest in the UK?
- How would adopting the single currency affect our financial services?
- Are business cycles and economic structures compatible so that we and others in Europe could live comfortably with euro interest rates on a permanent basis?
- If problems do emerge, is there sufficient flexibility to deal with them?
- Will joining EMU help to promote higher growth, stability and a lasting increase in jobs?

Of these, most economists believe that the third condition, convergence of economic cycles and business structures, is the most important and will be the most difficult to achieve on a genuine basis. In 1999, Britain's economy was at a more advanced stage of the economic cycle than most EMU members, while the UK economy has traditionally been more interest-rate sensitive (because of a higher proportion of variable rate debt, notably mortgages).

Gambling with the pound

As the euro looms, the Sun asks a crucial question. It is the question we never dreamed we would ask, but we have been forced to think the unthinkable. And today the *Sun* demands:

IS TONY BLAIR THE MOST DANGEROUS MAN IN BRITAIN?

In most respects he is a fine premier, but he seems determined to scrap the pound and take Britain into the European single currency. And that, we believe, will be the biggest gamble any prime minister has ever taken.

The result could be disastrous for this country. That is why the *Sun* has vowed to fight it all the way.

Blair is a charming, persuasive politician. We like him. He as the potential to be a truly great prime minister. He thinks fast and outflanks opponents with a smile that conceals a touch of steel. These are the qualities which propelled him to election triumph and now make him the world's most popular politician.

Many of his actions, like peace moves in Northern Ireland and ruthlessly modernizing Labour, have been applauded by *Sun* readers. Other decisions, like cutting the age for gay sex to 16, fly in the face of public opinion. But they pale compared to the biggest issue of all: our membership of the single currency.

Eleven key European states are committed to this dangerous gamble which could put the world economy in peril. Their decision, taken under Mr Blair's EU presidency, removes any doubt that the euro will be up and running next January. The prime minister, once a sceptic and now a convert, has decided Britain cannot afford to be left out. He has decided the pound must go and, almost imperceptibly, he has shifted his stance to become an advocate for the revolution.

The *Sun* backed him at the election because we believed he was the best man for the job. We still believe that. But our support, as we made plain at the time, did not give him a blank cheque. If he is determined to propel us into the single currency, he will find the *Sun* a determined opponent.

We know Blair has had his doubts. He agrees with President Clinton that Europe's outdated but powerful labour and welfare lobbies could wreck the euro. He knows British and German industrialists have grave fears about a system which could lead to economic disaster.

Blair also knows that the majority of British voters – and perhaps most other EU countries – are deeply unhappy about this gigantic experiment. But he has decided to use his popularity to cajole, seduce and persuade the voters to back him.

Why? Maybe it is because Germany's Chancellor Kohl has told him on the sly: 'Young Tony, you can be the leader of Europe.' Maybe Blair feels he can get away with sliding us into the euro because there has been no serious debate on the matter.

Well, there is now. The *Sun* will not flinch from opposing the euro. We are against it economically, politically and constitutionally.

WE WILL FIGHT, FIGHT, FIGHT.

And whatever happens, we hope people will use the words of the greatest of all Englishmen, Winston Churchill, and say...

THIS WAS THEIR FINEST HOUR.

The Sun, 24 June 1998

In February 1999, the government published its *National Changeover Plan* to the euro, although again without setting a firm timetable for entry. Its policy, it said, was 'prepare and decide'. If the government decided in favour of entry, it said, a referendum could take place four months later. The process of entering EMU would take a further 24–30 months, at the end of which there would be a six-month conversion period from sterling to euro notes and coins.

The battle over euro entry promises to be a fascinating one:

- Many (but not all) larger businesses favour entry because of the savings in transaction costs, and because it will make it easier for them to do business in Europe with a single currency – and therefore no exchange rate risk (although that risk will remain outside Europe).
- Smaller businesses are, in general, more sceptical. Many do not have transaction costs with Europe.
- Public opinion is deeply divided for both economic and political reasons.

KEY WORDS

European Union	European economic and
European Coal and Steel	monetary union
Community	Social protocol
Treaty of Rome	Trade creation
European Economic	Trade diversion
Community	Second-best solution
European Free Trade	Werner committee
Association	Bretton Woods
Common Agricultural Policy	European Monetary System
Common external tariff	Exchange rate mechanism
Customs union	European Currency Unit
Single European Act	Delors report
Single market	Euro
Common market	Maastricht criteria
Treaty on European Union	Transaction costs
	Optimum currency areas

Further reading
Currie, D., *The Pros and Cons of EMU*, HM Treasury,1997.
Hill, B., Chapters 6 and 7 in *The European Union*, 3rd edn, Heinemann Educational, 1998.
Smith, D., *Eurofutures*, Capstone, 1997.
Smith, D., *Will Europe Work?*, Social Market Foundation/Profile Books, 1999.

Useful websites
European Central Bank: www.ecb.int
European Commission: //europa.eu.int

Essay topics
1. Assume the UK joins a monetary union with a single European currency. Examine the likely economic effects of this on:
   (a) the UK's pattern of trade [30 marks]
   (b) EU consumers and producers [40 marks]
   (c) UK macroeconomic management. [30 marks]
   [University of London Examinations and Assessment Council 1997]
2. (a) Examine the costs and benefits for firms and consumers of a country being part of a free trade area. [60 marks]
   (b) What might be the economic advantages and disadvantages for a member of the EU which does not join the European monetary union? [40 marks] [University of London Examinations and Assessment Council 1998]

Data response question
The following is adapted from an article entitled 'EMU to make uncertain start', prepared by Patrick Foley for publication in *Lloyds Bank Economic Bulletin* in February 1998. Read the piece and then answer the questions that follow.

The UK's trade with Europe

The UK now faces a situation where over half of its goods exports, and one-third of its services exports, go to the euro area (see the charts). Total exports to that region account for around 15 per cent of the UK's GDP. The UK will rely on this same bloc for 55 per cent of its goods imports and 36 per cent of its services imports. Changes in the economic status of the euro area or in the euro/sterling exchange rate will thus have a profound impact on the UK economy.

Goods exports, 1996
(Total: £166bn)

Rest of
world
31%

EU 11
52%

USA
12%

'Outs'
5%

Services exports, 1996
(Total: £51bn)

Rest of
world
42%

EU 11
33%

'Outs'
4%

USA
21%

Source: ONS

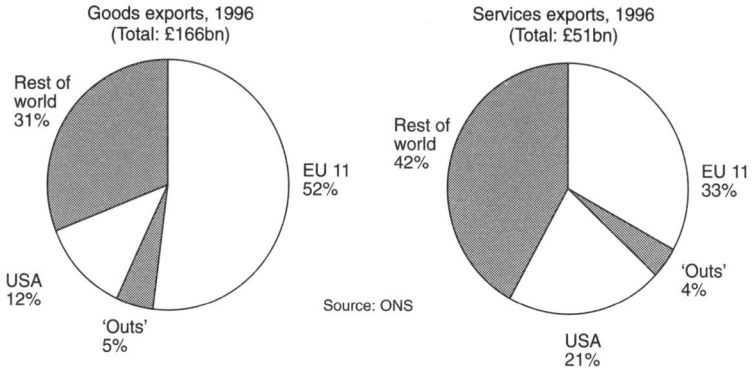

The European Central Bank is likely to follow a policy of benign neglect towards the external value of the euro, which may lead to misalignments against other currencies including those of the 'outs'. Although an ERM 2 is planned for those 'outs' who wish to join (and will presumably be a criterion for future entry), it is envisaged as having very wide bands, with frequent realignments if necessary. Furthermore, the onus for defending parities in this new ERM will lie fully with the central banks of the 'outs'. The ECB is under no obligation to take any action.

The 'out' countries face a dilemma. Given free capital mobility across EU borders, they can either follow an independent monetary policy or try to fix their exchange rates against the euro.

At present the UK is targeting domestic inflation and ignoring the exchange rate (except insofar as its level or rate of change has implications for inflation). Consequently, interest rates are much higher than in the rest of Europe, sterling is strong and the slowdown is concentrated in manufacturing.

Apart from having to deal with exchange rate fluctuations (perhaps severe) against its biggest market, UK industry will face another difficulty. Formation of a single currency area will in time cause profound shifts in the structure of European industry. These shifts may disadvantage businesses based in the 'out' countries.

One effect of the creation of the euro area will be a shift in foreign direct investment flows away from the 'outs' and towards the 'ins'. The UK, in particular amongst the 'outs', has been a major recipient of foreign direct investment in recent years, with inflows second only to those of the USA and China.

A second likely effect of the creation of the euro area will in time be a substantial relocation of European business, as companies take advantage of increasing returns by focusing production in one area from which to serve the entire euro area and to form clusters of activity with similar companies. Businesses from the same sector benefit from locating together for three principal reasons:

- skilled labour market pooling
- the development of specialized local suppliers
- technological spillovers from one firm to others.

Reduced transaction costs for trade across national borders within the euro area will encourage the development of business clusters in Europe.

Evidence shows that European business sectors are much less clustered in specific areas than are their US counterparts. Over time this is likely to change. Furthermore, increasing returns to clustering imply that whichever region gains an initial cost advantage through this process tends to sustain and grow that advantage – accidents of history determine future industrial structure.

1. How significant is the UK's trade with the euro area? [2 marks]
2. Explain the sentence 'The ECB is likely to follow a policy of benign neglect towards the external value of the euro, which may lead to substantial misalignments against other currencies, including those of the 'outs'. [5 marks]
3. (a) Which are the 'out' countries? [3 marks]
   (b) Why do the 'out' countries have to choose between an independent monetary policy and fixing their exchange rate against the euro? [4 marks]
4. What benefits can firms gain from locating near to other firms in the same industry? [4 marks]
5. Assess whether staying out of the single currency will reduce UK output and employment. [7 marks]

Conclusion

This book has tried, as before, to bring out the multi-faceted nature of economic policy in the UK. Economic policy is not all about the next change in interest rates, or the Chancellor's annual budget, however important they might be. Macroeconomic policy may capture the headlines but, as I have tried to show, microeconomic policy is often equally important. Currently, UK economic policy is heavy on microeconomics, with the New Deal, the working families tax credit and the government's competition and productivity agendas all very good examples of this.

There are three things to emphasize. One is that the policy emphasis does change over time. In the 1970s and 80s, such was the concern over inflation, even hyper-inflation, that other economic goals, notably full employment, appeared to be relegated. Maintaining sound finances became the priority. But sound finances, while necessary, can never be the sole aim of economic policy. Achieving the highest possible level of employment, and the fastest sustainable increase in living standards, are ultimately what it is all about.

The second point is that a book of this size can never be comprehensive. Mention of the word sustainable in the preceding paragraph reminds me that that there is little in this book about the use of economic instruments, such as taxation, for environmental purposes. That may be an issue which rises in importance over the next few years.

Finally, as noted in the introduction, economics is a living, evolving subject, and this is particularly the case for economic policy. Change makes it a challenging subject to teach, and to keep abreast of, but it also makes it all the more rewarding. Policy evolves, but sometimes it comes around in circles. Knowing what is new, and what is recycled, is part of the fun. The interaction of politics and economics, which is the essence of economic policy, is fascinating, and deserves the widest possible audience. Newspaper articles, including my own, are one source of information and analysis. I am also happy to enter into dialogue (e-mail: david.smith@sunday-times.co.uk), although neither I nor your teachers would want me to be answering your essay questions!

In a wider sense, economic policy and its consequences are all around us. Everybody should have a basic grounding in how the process works.

Index

Lo
nc
tl